ANOTHER PART
OF THE FOREST

ALSO BY LILLIAN HELLMAN

REGINA, *to Marcus:* Let's take our lunch and go on a picnic, just you and me.   GRAPHIC HOUSE PHOTO

ANOTHER PART *of the* FOREST

A PLAY IN THREE ACTS

By Lillian Hellman

New York · The Viking Press · 1947

812.5
N 36 a
59524
Nov. 1967

*The amateur acting rights of this play are controlled
exclusively by the Dramatists Play Service, Inc., 6 East
39th Street, New York 16, New York, without whose
permission in writing no performance of it may be
given.*

*All inquiries concerning stock production of this play
should be addressed to Samuel French, 25 West 45th
Street, New York 19, N. Y.*

SET IN LINOTYPE AND MONOTYPE BASKERVILLE AND
A.T.F. CASLON OPEN FACE TYPES

PRINTED IN U.S.A. BY VAIL-BALLOU PRESS, INC.;
BOUND BY H. WOLFF BOOK MANUFACTURING CO.

FOR MY GOOD FRIEND

GREGORY ZILBOORG

KERMIT BLOOMGARDEN PRESENTS
LILLIAN HELLMAN'S NEW PLAY

Another Part of the Forest

CAST

(IN ORDER OF THEIR APPEARANCE)

REGINA HUBBARD	Patricia Neal
JOHN BAGTRY	Bartlett Robinson
LAVINIA HUBBARD	Mildred Dunnock
CORALEE	Beatrice Thompson
MARCUS HUBBARD	Percy Waram
BENJAMIN HUBBARD	Leo Genn
JACOB	Stanley Greene
OSCAR HUBBARD	Scott McKay
SIMON ISHAM	Owen Coll
BIRDIE BAGTRY	Margaret Phillips
HAROLD PENNIMAN	Paul Ford
GILBERT JUGGER	Gene O'Donnell
LAURETTE SINCEE	Jean Hagen

The play was directed by Miss Hellman.

The settings were designed by Jo Mielziner.

Opened at the Fulton Theatre on the night of November 20, 1946.

SYNOPSIS OF SCENES

ACT ONE: *A Sunday morning in June 1880, the Alabama town of Bowden, the side portico of the Hubbard house.*

ACT TWO: *The next evening, the living room of the Hubbard house.*

ACT THREE: *Early the next morning, the side portico of the Hubbard house.*

Throughout the play, in the stage directions, left and right mean audience's left and right.

ANOTHER PART
OF THE FOREST

ACT ONE

SCENE: *The side portico of the Hubbard house, a Sunday morning in the summer of 1880 in the Alabama town of Bowden. The portico leads into the living room by back center French doors. On the right side of the portico is an old wing of the house. An exterior staircase to this wing leads to an upper porch off which are the bedrooms of the house and behind the staircase are the back gardens and the kitchen quarters. Under the second-story porch is a door leading to the dining room of the house, and a back door leading to the kitchen. The other side of the portico leads to a lawn which faces the town's main street. The main part of the house, built in the 1850's, is Southern Greek. It is not a great mansion but it is a good house built by a man of taste from whom Marcus Hubbard bought it after the Civil War. There is not much furniture on the portico: two chairs and a table at one end, one comfortable chair and a table at the other end. Twin heads of Aristotle are on high pedestals. There is something too austere, too pretended Greek about the portico, as if it followed one man's eccentric taste and was not designed to be comfortable for anyone else.*

3

As the curtain rises, Regina Hubbard, a handsome girl of twenty, is standing looking down at John Bagtry. Regina has on a pretty negligee thrown over a night-gown. Her hair is pinned high, as if she had pinned it up quickly. John Bagtry is a man of thirty-six with a sad, worn face. He is dressed in shabby riding shirt and Confederate Cavalry pants.

REGINA, *after a long silence:* Where were you going?

JOHN, *he has a soft, easy voice:* And what you doing awake so early?

REGINA: Watching for you. But you tried not to hear me when I called you. I called you three times before you turned.

JOHN: I didn't think this was the place or the hour for us to be meeting together. *Looks around nervously.* We'll be waking your folks. You out here in your wrapper! That would make a pretty scandal, honey—

REGINA, *impatiently:* Nobody's awake. And I don't care. Why didn't you—

JOHN, *quickly, gaily:* Oh, your Mama's up all right. I saw her and your Coralee going into nigger church. I bowed to her—

REGINA, *softly:* Why didn't you meet me last night?

JOHN, *after a second:* I couldn't. And I didn't know how to send word.

REGINA: Why couldn't you? Plantation folks giving balls again? Or fancy dress parties?

JOHN, *smiles:* I haven't been to a party since I was sixteen years old, Regina. The Bacons gave the last ball I ever remember, to celebrate the opening of the war and say good-bye to us—

REGINA: You've told me about it. Why couldn't you come last night?

JOHN: I couldn't leave Aunt Clara and Cousin Birdie. They wanted to sit out and talk after supper, and I couldn't.

REGINA, *slowly:* They wanted to talk? And so they made you stay?

JOHN: No, they didn't *make* me. They're lonely, Regina, and I'm not with them much, since you and I—

REGINA: Why should you be with them? When I want to meet you, I go and do it.

JOHN: Things are different with us. Everything is bad. This summer is the worst, I guess, in all the years. They are lonely—

REGINA: It's not the first time you didn't come. And you think I shouldn't be angry, and take you back the next day. It would be better if you lied to me where you were. This way it's just insulting to me. Better if you lied.

JOHN: Lie? Why would I lie?

REGINA: Better if you said you were with another woman. But not meeting me because of those two mummies—

JOHN, *softly:* I like them, Regina. And they don't go around raising their voices in anger on an early Sunday day.

REGINA: I don't want you to tell me about the differences in your family and mine.

JOHN, *stares at her:* I've never done that. Never.

REGINA: That's what you always mean when you say I'm screaming.

JOHN, *sharply:* I mean no such thing. I said only that I stayed with Aunt Clara and Cousin Birdie last night. And I'll do it again. *Desperately:* Look, honey, I didn't mean not to come to meet you. But I've lived on them for fifteen years. They're good to me. They share with me the little they got, and I don't give back anything to them—

REGINA, *tensely:* I'm getting sick of them. They've got to know about you and me some day soon. I think I'm going to sashay right up to that sacred plantation grass and tell them the war's over, the old times are finished, and so are they. I'm going to tell them to stay out of my way—

JOHN, *sharply:* They've never mentioned you, Regina.

REGINA: That's good breeding: to know about something and not talk about it?

JOHN: I don't know about good breeding.

REGINA, *turns to him:* They think they do. Your Cousin Birdie's never done more than say good morning in all these years—when she knows full well who I am and who Papa is. Knows full well he could buy and sell Lionnet on the same morning, its cotton and its women with it—

JOHN, *takes her arm, very sharply:* I would not like to hear anybody talk that way again. No, I wouldn't.

REGINA, *pleadingly, softly:* I'm sorry, I'm sorry, I'm sorry. I give you my apology. I'm sorry, darling.

JOHN: We shouldn't be—

REGINA, *runs to him, takes his arm:* I'm never going to be mean again, never going to talk mean— Look, honey, I was mad about last night because I wanted to tell you about my plan. I've been thinking about it for months, and I've got Papa almost ready for it. But I can't tell it to you tonight because Papa makes me read to him every Sunday. But late tomorrow night, after Papa's music—it's over early—please, darling, tomorrow night—tomorrow night— *She clings to him.*

JOHN, *turns to her:* Regina, we mustn't. We mustn't any more. It's not right for you, honey, we're a scandal now. I'm no good for you. I'm too old, I'm—

REGINA, *clinging to him, impatient:* Why do you say that? A man at thirty-six talking that way? It comes from hanging around this town and your kinfolk.

JOHN: I was only good once—in a war. Some men shouldn't ever come home from a war. You know something? It's the only time I was happy.

REGINA, *draws away from him, wearily:* Oh, don't tell

me that again. You and your damn war. Wasn't it silly to be happy when you knew you were going to lose?

JOHN: You think it is silly? You think we all were? Of course you do. In this house you couldn't think anything else. *She draws back.* And now *I'm* sorry. That was most rude. It's late, honey.

REGINA, *quickly:* You haven't even asked me about my plan.

JOHN: I have a plan, too. I have a letter from Cod Carter. He's in Brazil. He's fighting down there, he says—

Lavinia Hubbard and Coralee appear from around the portico, as if coming from street. John stares at them, draws back nervously. Regina watches him, amused. Lavinia Hubbard is a woman of about fifty-eight, stooped, thin, delicate-looking. She has a sweet, high voice and a distracted, nervous way of speaking. Coralee is a sturdy Negro woman of about forty-five. She is holding a parasol over Lavinia. John steps forward. Coralee folds parasol, stares at Regina's costume, exits under porch to kitchen.

LAVINIA, *as if this were an ordinary morning scene:* Morning, Captain Bagtry. Been for a nice little stroll?

JOHN, *quickly:* Morning, Mrs. Hubbard. No, ma'am. I was just riding by and glimpsed Miss Regina—

LAVINIA, *nods:* That's nice. Coralee and I been to our church. The colored folks said a prayer for me and a little song. It's my birthday.

JOHN: Congratulations, ma'am. I sure give you my good wishes.

LAVINIA: Thank you, sir. And later I'm going back to the second service. And I know a secret: they're going to give me a cake. Ain't that lovely of them, and me undeserving? *Looks up at him:* I always go to the colored church. I ain't been to a white church in years. Most people don't like my doing it, I'm sure, but I got my good reasons—

REGINA: All right, Mama.

LAVINIA: There's got to be one little thing you do that you want to do, all by yourself you want to do it.

REGINA, *sharply:* All right, Mama.

LAVINIA, *hurries toward the doors of the living room:* Oh. Sorry. *At the door of living room, looks back at John:* I remember you and your cousins the day you left town for war. I blew you a kiss. Course we were living in our little house then and you didn't know. But I blew you all a kiss.

JOHN, *very pleased:* I'm glad to know it, ma'am. It was a great day. A hot day— You know something, ma'am? It was my birthday, too, that day. I was sixteen, and my cousins not much older. My birthday. Isn't that a coincidence, ma'am?

REGINA: Why?

JOHN, *lamely:* Because it's your Mama's birthday today.

LAVINIA: And you know something else, Captain Bagtry? Tomorrow's my wedding anniversary day. Your birthday, my birthday, and a wedding anniversary day.

REGINA, *very sharply:* All right, Mama.

Marcus Hubbard opens the door of his bedroom and appears on the upper porch. He is a strong-looking man of sixty-three, with a soft voice of tone and depth. He speaks slowly, as if he put value on the words.

MARCUS: Who's speaking on the porch?

At the sound of his voice Lavinia hurries into the house. John draws back into the living-room doors. Regina comes forward.

REGINA: I'm down here, Papa.

MARCUS: Morning, darling. Waiting for me?

REGINA: Er. Mama's just been to church.

MARCUS: Of course—where else would she go? Wait. Have your first coffee with me. *He exits into his room.*

REGINA, *amused at John's nervous movements, takes his arm:* I want you to meet Papa. Not now. But soon.

JOHN: I know your Papa. I'm in and out of your store—

REGINA: I want you to come *here.* I guess no Bagtry ever been inside our house. But would your Aunt Clara and your Cousin Birdie allow you to come, do you reckon?

JOHN: Allow me? I didn't think that was the way it was. I thought your Papa didn't want anybody here—

REGINA: He doesn't. But I'll find a way. Will you meet me tomorrow night, same place? Darling, darling, please. Please. *She pulls him toward her. He hesitates for a second. Then he takes her in his arms, kisses her with great feeling. She smiles.* Meet me?

JOHN, *softly:* I always do. No matter what I say or think, I always do.

He kisses her again. Then he runs off. She stands for a minute staring after him. Then, from the street side of the lawn, Benjamin Hubbard appears. He is followed by Jacob carrying a small valise and three boxes. Jacob is a tall, thin Negro of about thirty. Ben is thirty-five: a powerful, calm man with a quiet manner.

REGINA, *amused:* Morning, Ben. Have a good trip?

BEN: Was that Bagtry?

REGINA: He said that was his name.

BEN: What you doing having men on the porch, you in your wrapper?

REGINA, *gaily:* Isn't it a pretty wrapper? Came from Chicago.

BEN, *pointing to boxes:* And so did these, on the mail train. They got your name on 'em. Belong to you?

REGINA, *giggling:* Writing can't lie. Specially writing in ink.

MARCUS, *reappears on balcony, calls down:* Coffee ready for me, darling?

REGINA, *gaily, smiling at Ben:* Going in to brew it myself, honey.

She disappears into house. Marcus comes forward on the porch, sees Ben and Jake.

MARCUS, *stares at Jake:* Jake, take the boxes in. *Jake starts in.* And put Mr. Benjamin's valise out of your hand. *Jake hesitates, looks puzzled. Ben stares up at Marcus. Then Jake puts valise down, exits.* How was the world of fashion, Benjamin?

BEN: I was only in it for twenty-four hours.

MARCUS: Ah. That isn't long enough.

BEN: You ordered me back.

MARCUS: What for?

BEN, *looks up, smiles:* The pleasure of it, I think.

MARCUS, *giggles:* Certainly. But what did I call the pleasure?

BEN: You said the books needed checking, and I was to be back to do them today.

MARCUS, *thinks:* Books? I wouldn't let you touch the books in my library, Benjamin. Certainly you know that.

BEN, *annoyed:* Books for the store. *Store. Bookkeeping. Accounts.*

MARCUS: Oh. But why today?

BEN: I don't know, Papa. I'd like to have stayed in Mobile. I had some business—

MARCUS, *clucks:* But I brought you back on a Sunday to look at store books. Now why did I do that? I must have had some reason. I'll think of it later. *He looks down, realizes Ben isn't going to answer.* What business did you have, Ben?

BEN: I wanted to invest two thousand dollars in Birmingham Coal, Incorporated. It will bring fifty thousand some day. There's coal there, and they're sending down men from the North with money for it— But I couldn't raise it. And you wouldn't lend it to me.

MARCUS: That why you went? That foolish old scheme of yours? I had hoped you went to Mobile for a lady.

BEN: No, sir. I have no lady.

MARCUS: I believe you. But certainly you went to the concert last night?

BEN: No, I didn't. I told you: I was trying to borrow the two thousand you wouldn't let me have.

MARCUS: Well, you must hear a good concert before you die.

Lavinia and Coralee enter from kitchen door.

MARCUS, *starts into his room:* Carry in your own valise, son. It is not seemly for a man to load his goods on other men, black or white.

Ben looks up, half annoyed, half amused. He picks up his valise, starts toward door as Coralee appears, carrying breakfast tray. Lavinia follows her. Ben watches them as Coralee puts tray on table. Lavinia, knowing that Marcus is on the balcony, but not knowing whether she should speak to him, helps Coralee by aimlessly fussing about with the tray.

LAVINIA, *to Ben:* Morning, son.

BEN: Morning, Mama.

LAVINIA: Pleasant trip?

BEN: No, unsuccessful.

LAVINIA: That's good, I'm sure. I mean— Morning, Marcus.

MARCUS: Coralee. I'll be right down. Lavinia, send everybody else to the dining room for breakfast. Go on, Lavinia.

He disappears. Lavinia spills coffee.

CORALEE, *quickly:* All right, Miss Viney. No harm. Go on in and have your breakfast before there's trouble.

LAVINIA: I was only trying—

Lavinia goes into living room as Marcus comes downstairs carrying a book. He goes immediately to table. Coralee pours coffee.

MARCUS: Who is down for breakfast?

CORALEE: I don't know.

LAVINIA, *reappears in living-room doorway:* Oh, Marcus, Colonel Isham is calling. Can he come out?

MARCUS: If he is capable of walking.

Colonel Isham, a man of sixty-five, appears in the doorway.

MARCUS: Colonel Isham.

ISHAM: You will forgive this too early visit?

MARCUS: You're in town for church?

ISHAM: I've come to see you. I was asked to come to see you.

MARCUS: To talk about bad cotton?

ISHAM: No, sir. I don't mix with a man's Sunday breakfast, to talk about cotton. I come to talk about your son Oscar.

MARCUS: Then you will need coffee.

ISHAM: Thank you, no. Two nights ago—

MARCUS: People like you don't drink coffee with people like me?

ISHAM: I've had coffee. Now, Mr. Hubbard—

MARCUS: Then come again when you haven't had it.

There is a pause. Slowly Isham comes to the table. Marcus smiles, pours a cup of coffee, hands it to Isham, who takes it and sits down.

ISHAM: Thank you. I have come here for your sake, Mr. Hubbard. There is dangerous feeling up in my town this morning—

MARCUS: Colonel, I hate conversations for my sake. Sunday is my day of study. I don't wish to sound rude but please say quickly what you have come about.

ISHAM, *smiles:* Mr. Hubbard, I'm too old to frighten.

MARCUS, *smiles:* And I should be a daring man to try it. You, one of our great heroes. Commanding the first Alabama troops at—

ISHAM, *sharply:* I am not interested in talking to you about the War Between the States, or about your personal war on the people of this state— Now, please listen to me. Two nights ago Sam Taylor in Roseville was badly beaten up. Last night fourteen people identified the night riders as the Cross boys, from over the line, and your son Oscar.

MARCUS, *shouts into the house:* Benjamin. Rope Oscar and bring him out here immediately. I told you fifteen years ago you were damn fools to let Klansmen ride around, carrying guns—

ISHAM: Were you frightened of our riding on you? I came here to tell you to make your son quit. He can thank me he's not swinging from a rope this minute. You have good reason to know there's not a man in this county wouldn't like to swing up anybody called Hubbard. I stopped my friends last night but I may not be able to stop them again. Tell him what patriots do is our business. But he's got no right to be riding down on anybody—

Ben, followed by Oscar, appears in the dining-room doorway. Oscar looks frightened, decides to be cute.

OSCAR: *Rope* me out. I can stand up, Papa. Never felt my Saturday night liquor that bad—

ISHAM, *ignoring Oscar, to Marcus:* Taylor is a good

man. He's got no money for treatment, got no job now, won't get one again.

MARCUS, *to Oscar:* Colonel Isham has just saved you from a lynching party. Should I thank him?

OSCAR, *terrified:* Lynching! What did— Colonel Isham —I—

ISHAM: I don't want to speak with you.

MARCUS: Who does?

OSCAR: But what did I—

MARCUS: Do I have to tell you that if you ever put on those robes again, or take a gun to any man— *Takes roll of bills from his pocket, throws it to Benjamin:* Count out five hundred dollars, Benjamin.

OSCAR, *very nervous:* You mean Taylor? I wasn't riding with the Klan boys. No, I wasn't. I was thinking about it, but—

BEN: No, he couldn't have been with them. He took me to the Mobile train, and the train was late, so we sat talking. He couldn't have got up to Roseville.

ISHAM: You say you're willing to swear to that, Mr. Benjamin? You sure you're willing to go against fourteen people identifying your brother—?

BEN: Oh, Oscar looks like anybody.

MARCUS, *smiles:* Give the money to Colonel Isham, Benjamin. Go away, Oscar. *Oscar exits through dining-room door.* Please use the money for Taylor.

ISHAM: We'll take care of him, Hubbard. Good day, sir.

MARCUS: You won't take care of him, because you can't. Learn to be poor, Isham, it has more dignity. Tell Taylor there will be a check each month. Tell him that my other son, Benjamin, wishes to make amends. Ben has a most charitable nature.

Isham hesitates, decides, takes the money, looks at it.

ISHAM: There is no need for so much. A hundred would be more proper.

MARCUS: Good day, Colonel. Don't give me lectures on propriety.

Isham starts to speak, changes his mind, exits left toward street. There is a pause. Ben looks at Marcus, drops the roll of money on Marcus's table.

BEN, *smiles:* You didn't like my story about Oscar?

MARCUS: Not much. Very loyal of you, however.

BEN: I like it.

MARCUS: Good. It's yours. Keep it. You must have one of your usual involved reasons for wanting it.

BEN: Five hundred dollars is a lot of money to a man who allows himself six dollars for a trip to Mobile.

MARCUS: Perhaps you're stingy.

BEN: You can't be much else on a salary of twenty dollars a week.

MARCUS: Is that all I pay you? Ah, well, you'll be better off when I—if and when I die. But I may not die; did I tell you, Benjamin?

Regina, Oscar and Lavinia appear from the living room. Regina hurries to Marcus.

REGINA: Forgive me, darling. I forgot your coffee.

Oscar is carrying a cup of coffee and a roll. Lavinia, who never sees anything, bumps into him. Oscar turns on her angrily.

OSCAR: Goodness sake, Mama. Watch where you going.

REGINA: Oscar's in a bad humor this morning. Oscar's got one of those faces shows everything.

LAVINIA, *to everybody—nobody pays any attention:* I'm sorry. I'm sure I didn't mean to—

MARCUS: Oscar has good reason for being in a bad humor. He owes me five hundred dollars.

Oscar's hand begins to shake on the cup. He rattles the spoon and saucer.

BEN: For God's sake sit down and stop rattling that cup.

OSCAR: Papa, you can't mean that— Ben told you where I was. I wasn't even—

MARCUS, *to Regina:* You look charming. New?

REGINA: No. But I *did* buy a few new dresses.

MARCUS: A few? I saw the boxes coming in.

OSCAR: Seven dresses. Seven, I counted them.

REGINA: Can you count up to seven now? And more coming next week, Papa.

MARCUS: What are you going to do with them, honey?

REGINA, *hesitates, then gaily:* Could we go for a walk?

BEN: You buying these clothes out of your allowance?

REGINA, *laughs:* Aren't you silly? How could I? There's a fur piece and a muff that cost three hundred dollars alone. They're charming, Papa, wait till you see them—

OSCAR, *delighted at the diversion in the conversation:* You really gone crazy? Nobody's ever worn furs in this climate since old lady Somers put that bear rug around her and jumped out the porch.

REGINA: I won't jump out the porch.

BEN: I will have to O.K. the bills, so would you tell me how much you've spent?

REGINA, *airily:* I don't know. I didn't even ask.

OSCAR, *shrilly:* Didn't even ask? Didn't even ask? You gone real crazy, acting like Miss Vanderbilt, whatever her name is—rich people up North don't act that way. They watch their money, and their fathers' money.

REGINA: Oh, that's not true. Those people in Chicago, just the other day, gave their daughter a hundred-thousand-dollar check for a trousseau—

BEN, *looks at her:* A trousseau? So that's what you're buying? I saw Horace Giddens in Mobile last evening, and he was mighty disappointed you haven't answered his letter about coming up for another visit here.

OSCAR: Hey, he wouldn't be bad for you, Regina—

BEN: He's in love with you. That was obvious when he was here. It's good society, that family, and rich. Solid, quiet rich.

OSCAR: And you'd get to like him. A lot of people get married not liking each other. Then, after marriage, they still don't like each other much, I guess—

BEN, *sharply:* Are you still drunk?

LAVINIA, *comes to life:* A wedding? That would be nice. I hope you make your plans right quick, Regina, because—

MARCUS, *very slowly:* What is all this, Regina?

LAVINIA: I didn't say anything. I was twisting my handkerchief—

REGINA: It's nothing, Papa, nothing. You know Ben. You know he wants me to marry money for him. I'm not even thinking about Giddens. I don't like him.

BEN: Certainly I want you to marry money. More than that— *She wheels around to stare at him.* You're twenty years old. You ought to be settled down. You been worrying us. *Pleased at the nervousness Regina is showing:* Isn't that so, Mama? Hasn't Regina been worrying you?

LAVINIA: I really don't know, son. I really couldn't say.

OSCAR: Well, I could say she's been worrying me. Many's the time I thought of taking action. Sashaying around as open as—

REGINA, *to Oscar:* Oh, shut up. *To Marcus:* Papa. You can't blame me if Ben thinks up one of his plans to annoy you, and Oscar chimes in like he always does. I bought the clothes because I—because I want to take a little trip. That's all, Papa.

MARCUS: A trip?

REGINA: All right. I'll send back the dresses. I don't know what all this talk's about. *Comes to him:* Spoiling your Sunday. Come on, darling. Let's take our lunch and go on a picnic, just you and me. We haven't done that in a long time.

MARCUS: No, not for a long time. *To Ben:* Something amuses you?

BEN: Yes. You and Regina.

MARCUS, *to Ben and Oscar:* The two of you have contrived to give me a bad morning. *To Oscar:* And you have cost me five hundred dollars. How much you drawing at the store?

OSCAR, *nervous but determined:* I was going to talk to you about that, Papa. I'm drawing sixteen a week. It ain't enough, Papa, because, well, I'm getting on and I want a little life of my own. I was going to ask you if you couldn't sort of make a little advance against a little raise—

MARCUS: You'll get eleven a week hereafter. Five dollars will go to repay me for the five hundred.

OSCAR: My God, Papa. You can't— Eleven a week! My

God, Papa— That wasn't what I meant. You mis-
understood me 'cause I wasn't talking clear. I wanted
a little *raise,* not a—

MARCUS, *to Ben, sharply:* Put aside your plans for your
sister's future. Spend with profit your time today going
over the store books. *Then, amused:* You'll find we
are short of cash. Call in some cotton loans or mortgages. *Giggles.* Then go to church.

LAVINIA, *delighted:* Want to come with me, Benjamin?
I'm going to my church, because they're saying a prayer
for my birthday. *To Marcus:* It's my birthday, Marcus.

MARCUS: Congratulations, Lavinia.

LAVINIA: Thank you. *Comes to Marcus:* We were going to talk today. You promised, Marcus—

MARCUS: I promised to talk? Talk about what?

LAVINIA, *amazed, worried:* Talk about what? You know,
Marcus. You promised last year, on my last birthday.
You said you were too busy that day, but this year you
said—

MARCUS: I'm still busy, my dear. Now you run and tell
Belle to make us up a fine picnic basket. *To Regina:*
And a good bottle of wine. I'll get it myself.

LAVINIA: But, Marcus, I been waiting since last year—

MARCUS: Get the lunch now. *She hesitates, looks frightened, goes toward kitchen door. To Regina:* I'll bring

my Aristotle. You'll read in English, I'll follow you in Greek. Shall we walk or drive?

REGINA, *smiling:* Let's walk. You get the wine and your books. I'll change my clothes— *He nods, smiles, goes into house. She stops to look at Ben, smiles:* You never going to learn, Ben. Been living with Papa for thirty-five years, and never going to learn.

OSCAR: Regina, you got a few hundred dollars to lend me? Wouldn't take me long to pay it back—

BEN: Learn what, honey?

OSCAR: Papa's sure hard on me. It's unnatural. If a stranger came in he'd think Papa didn't like me, his own son.

REGINA, *turns to Oscar:* You want some money? If you had any sense, you'd know how to get it: just tell Papa *Ben* don't want you to have it. You'll get it. *To Ben:* You ain't smart for a man who wants to get somewhere. You should have figured out long ago that Papa's going to do just whatever you tell him not to do, unless *I* tell him to do it. *Pats his shoulder.* Goodness gracious, that's been working for the whole twenty years I been on earth.

BEN, *to Regina:* You are right, and you're smart. You must give me a full lecture on Papa some day; tell me why he's so good to you, how you manage, and so on.

REGINA, *laughs:* I'm busy now, taking him on a picnic.

BEN: Oh, not now. Too hot for lectures. We'll wait for

a winter night. Before the fire. I'll sit opposite you and you'll talk and I'll listen. And I'll think many things, like how you used to be a beauty but at fifty years your face got worn and sour. Papa'll still be living, and he'll interrupt us, the way he does even now: he'll call from upstairs to have you come and put him to bed. And you'll get up to go, wondering how the years went by— *Sharply:* Because, as you say, he's most devoted to you, and he's going to keep you right here with him, all his long life.

REGINA, *angrily:* He's not going to keep me here. And don't you think he is. I'm going away. I'm going to Chicago— *Ben gets up, stares at her. Oscar looks up. She catches herself:* Oh, well, I guess you'd have to know. But I wanted him to promise before you began any interfering— I'm going for a trip, and a nice long trip. So you're wrong, honey.

BEN, *slowly:* He's consented to the trip?

REGINA, *giggles:* No. But he will by the time the picnic's over.

OSCAR: Chicago? You sure got Mama's blood. Little while now, and you're going to be just as crazy as Mama.

REGINA, *to Ben:* And the trip's going to cost a lot of money. I got books from hotels, and I know. But you'll be working hard in the store and sending it on to me—

BEN: You could always come home occasionally and go on another picnic. *Comes up to her:* This time I don't think so. Papa didn't just get mad about you and

Horace Giddens. Papa got mad about you and any man, or any place that ain't near him. I wouldn't like to be in the house, for example, the day he ever hears the gossip about you and Bagtry— *Sharply:* Or is Bagtry going to Chicago—

REGINA, *tensely, softly:* Be still, Ben.

OSCAR: And everybody sure is gossiping. Laurette even heard it up in Roseville. I said there's nothing between you. I wouldn't believe it. But if ever I thought there was I'd ride over to Lionnet, carrying a gun. I sure would—

REGINA, *carefully:* And the day you do I'll be right behind you. It'll be your last ride, darling.

OSCAR, *backing away:* All right, all right, I was joking. Everybody's talking so wild today—

REGINA, *turns back to Ben:* Look, Ben, don't start anything. I'll get you in trouble if you do.

BEN: I believe you.

REGINA: Wish me luck. I got a hard day's work ahead. *She goes up steps to upper porch and into her room.*

OSCAR, *yawns:* Where she going?

BEN: Try to keep awake. Why did you beat up Sam Taylor?

OSCAR, *after a second, sulkily:* He's a no-good carpet-bagger.

BEN, *wearily:* All right. Let's try again. Why did you beat up Sam Taylor?

OSCAR: He tried to make evening appointments with Laurette. He tried it twice. I told him the first time, and I told her too.

BEN: Is Laurette the little whore you've been courting?

OSCAR, *slowly, tensely:* Take that back, Ben. Take back that word. *Ben laughs. Oscar advances toward him, very angry:* I don't let any man—

BEN: Now listen to me, you clown. You put away your gun and keep it away. If those fools in your Klan want to beat up niggers and carpetbaggers, you let 'em do it. But you're not going to make this county dangerous to me, or dangerous to the business. We had a hard enough time making them forget Papa made too much money out of the war, and I ain't ever been sure they forgot it.

OSCAR: Course they haven't forgot it. Every time any-body has two drinks, or you call up another loan, there's plenty of talk, and plenty of hints I don't understand. *Rises.* If I had been old enough to fight in the war, you just bet I'd been right there, and not like you, bought off. I'm a Southerner. And when I see an old carpet-bagger or upstart nigger, why, I feel like taking revenge.

BEN: For what? Because Papa got rich on them? *Very sharply:* Put away that gun, sonny, and keep it put away, you hear me?

OSCAR, *frightened:* All right, all right. I want to thank

you. I forgot. For saying that I was talking to you on the train. Thanks, Ben.

BEN: I wasn't lying for you. I was trying to save five hundred dollars.

OSCAR, *hurt:* Oh. Guess I should have known. *Sighs:* How'm I ever going to pay it back? I'm in a mess. I— Ben, help me, will you? I'm deeply and sincerely in love.

BEN: Go give yourself a cooling sponge bath.

OSCAR: I want to marry Laurette. I was going to ask Papa to advance me a little money, so we could ship on down to New Orleans. He's going to leave money when he dies, plenty of it. I just want a little of mine now, and I'll go away—

BEN: He won't leave much. Not at this rate. He's spent forty thousand on nothing in the last six months.

OSCAR: My God, forty thousand and us slaving away in the store! And that's the way it's always going to be. I'm telling you: I'm taking Laurette and I'm going. Laurette's a fine girl. Hasn't looked at another man for a year.

BEN: Well, she better take them up again if you're going away. *You* can't earn a living.

Jake appears from the living room.

JAKE: Mr. Ben, a lady who says she doesn't want to say her name, she would like to speak with you. She's in the front hall, waiting.

BEN: Who? Who is it?

JAKE: Miss Birdie Bagtry.

Ben and Oscar turn in surprise.

BEN, *after a minute:* Wants to see *me*?   *Jake nods vigorously.* Bring her out. *Jake exits.*

OSCAR: Now what do you think of that? What's she want to come here for? To see *you*?   *Giggles.* What you been up to, boy?

BEN: Maybe she's come to look at you. Didn't you tell me she once gave you a glass of lemonade?

OSCAR: Did she?

BEN: I don't know. I only know that you told me so.

OSCAR: Then I guess it happened.

BEN: That doesn't necessarily follow.

OSCAR: Well, it was true. I was pushing a lame horse past Lionnet. I was lame myself from something or other—

BEN: Laurette Sincee?

OSCAR: I told you once, stop that. I am in love with Laurette, deeply and sincerely.

BEN: Better you'd stayed for the lemonade and fallen in love with Lionnet's cotton-fields.

OSCAR: Oh, this girl's supposed to be awfully silly. Melty-mush-silly. *Smiles:* That's what Laurette calls people like that. Melty-mush-silly.

BEN: She's witty, Laurette, eh? *Jake appears in the living-room door followed by a slight, pretty, faded-looking girl of twenty. Her clothes are seedy, her face is worn and frightened.* Good morning, ma'am.

OSCAR, *with charm:* Well, hello there, Miss Birdie!

BIRDIE, *bows:* Mr. Benjamin. And morning to you, Mr. Oscar. *Nervously:* We haven't seen you in many a long day. You haven't been hunting lately?

OSCAR: Oh, my time's been taken up with so many things, haven't had much chance.

BIRDIE *nods:* I know, you gentlemen in business. Please, you all, forgive my coming to your house, particularly on this day of privacy. I'll just take a few minutes and—

OSCAR: Excuse me, Miss Birdie. Hope you'll come again. *He starts toward room.*

BEN: Wait inside, Oscar. *Oscar turns to stare at him, then shrugs, disappears. To Birdie:* Please.

BIRDIE, *sits down:* Yes, sir. Thank you.

BEN: Can I get you coffee?

BIRDIE: No, sir. Thank you. You see, I only got a few minutes before Mama begins wondering. I'm sorry to worry you here, but I couldn't come to see you in the store, because then the whole town would know, wouldn't they? And my Mama and Cousin John would just about— *Giggles nervously.* Isn't that so, Mr. Benjamin?

BEN: Isn't what so?

BIRDIE, *very nervous:* About knowing. I must apologize for disturbing— Oh, I said that before. It's not good manners to take up all your time saying how sorry I am to take up all your time, now is it? *Giggles.* Oh, and I'm doing that again, too. Mama says I say everything in a question. Oh.

BEN: What do you want to talk to me about, Miss Birdie?

BIRDIE: Yes. *Rises. Desperately:* Mr. Benjamin, we're having a mighty bad time. It can't go on. It got so bad that last month Mama didn't want to do it, but she did it, and it was just awful for her.

BEN, *after a second, politely:* Did what?

BIRDIE: Went all the way to Natchez, just to keep from going to our kinfolk in Mobile. Course they're so poor now they couldn't have done anything anyway, but just to keep them from knowing she went all the way to Natchez.

BEN: Really?

BIRDIE: Yes, sir, all the way by herself. But they said they just couldn't. They said they'd like to, for Papa's dead sake and Grandpapa's, but they just couldn't. Mama said she didn't want it for anybody's sake, not like that, not for those reasons—well, you know Mama, Mr. Benjamin.

BEN: No, I don't.

BIRDIE: Oh. Well, I don't blame her, although . . . No, when everything else is gone, Mama says you at least got pride left. She did it to save me, Mr. Benjamin, the trip, I mean. I was such a ninny, being born when I did, and growing up in the wrong time. I'm much younger than my brothers. I mean I am younger, if they were living. But it didn't do any good.

BEN: I beg your pardon?

BIRDIE: The trip to Natchez. It didn't do any good.

BEN: What kind of good didn't it do? *She looks puzzled.* Why did your Mama make the trip?

BIRDIE: To borrow money on the cotton. Or on the land—*softly*—or even to sell the pictures, or the silver. But they said they couldn't: that everybody was raising cotton that nobody else wanted. I don't understand that. I thought people always wanted cotton.

BEN: They will again in fifty years.

BIRDIE, *after a pause:* Oh. Fifty years. *Smiles sadly.* Well, I guess we can't wait that long. The truth is, we can't pay or support our people, Mr. Benjamin, we can't— Well, it's just killing my Mama. And my Cousin John, he wants to go away.

BEN: Where does he want to go?

BIRDIE: Away from here. *Tense, very frightened:* Forgive me. Would you, I mean your father and you, would you lend money on our cotton, or land, or—

BEN: Your Cousin John, does he want to go to New York or Chicago, perhaps? Has he spoken of going to Chicago?

BIRDIE: Oh dear, no. There's no war going on in Chicago.

BEN: I beg your pardon?

BIRDIE: A war. He wants to go back to war. Mama says she can even understand that. She says there isn't any life for our boys any more.

BEN: I see. Where will Captain Bagtry find a war?

BIRDIE: There's something going on in Brazil, John says. He looked it up in the paper, and he's got a map.

BEN: Brazil. Is there a nice war going on in Brazil?

BIRDIE: Yes. I think so. *Eagerly:* You see, that was one of the things Mama was going to do with the money. Pay all our people and give John the carfare. He can earn a lot in Brazil, he can be a general. *Pauses, breathes:* Now about the loan, Mr. Benjamin—

BEN: You will inherit Lionnet?

BIRDIE: Me? Er. Yes. You mean if Mama were to— You mustn't believe those old stories. Mama's not so sick that a little good care and— *Very embarrassed:* I'm sorry.

BEN: You don't want your Mama to know you've come here?

BIRDIE: Oh, no, no. She'd never forgive me, rather die—

BEN, *laughs:* To think you had come to us.

BIRDIE: I didn't mean that. I am so sorry. I didn't—

BEN: You have not offended me, ma'am. I only ask because as I understand it you don't own Lionnet, your Mama does. But you don't want her to know about the loan. And so who would sign for it?

BIRDIE, *stares at him:* I would. Oh. You mean you can't sign for what you don't own. Oh. I see. I hadn't thought of that. Oh. That's how much of a ninny I am. Forgive me for bothering you. I shouldn't have. I'm sorry I just ruined your Sunday morning. Good day, sir.

BEN, *goes to dining-room door:* Oscar, Oscar, I know you want to walk Miss Bagtry home.

BIRDIE: Oh, no. Thank you. I—

OSCAR, *calling, offstage:* I have an appointment. I'm late.

BIRDIE, *embarrassed:* Please, sir—

BEN, *to Birdie:* How much of a loan were you thinking about?

BIRDIE: Five thousand dollars. It would take that much to pay our people and buy seed and pay debts and— But I guess I was as foolish about that as—

BEN: You know, of course, that all loans from our company are made by my father. I only work for him. Yours is good cotton and good land. But you don't own it. That makes it hard. It's very unusual, but perhaps I could think of some way to accommodate you. A promise from you, in a letter—

BIRDIE, *delighted:* Oh. Oh. Of course, I'd make the promise.

BEN: Why don't you talk to my father yourself? I'll tell him what it's all about, and you come back this afternoon—

BIRDIE, *backing away:* Oh, no. I couldn't say all that today again. I just couldn't— *Softly:* That's silly. Of course I could. What time will I come?

BEN: I have a pleasanter idea. Come tomorrow evening. Once a month my father has a music evening with musicians from Mobile to play on the violin, and flatter him. He's always in a good humor after his music. Come in then, Miss Birdie, and please invite Captain Bagtry to escort you.

BIRDIE: You really think there's any chance? Your Papa would— And my Mama wouldn't ever have to find out?

BEN, *bows:* I will do my best for you before you come.

BIRDIE, *after a second, with determination:* Thank you very much. I will be most pleased to come. Imagine having a concert right in your own house! I just love music. *Oscar appears in the door, stares angrily at Ben.* Thank you for your courtesy in offering to walk me back, Mr. Oscar. And thank you, Mr. Benjamin. *Birdie smiles happily, moves quickly off.*

OSCAR, *comes close to Ben, softly, very angry:* What the hell's the matter with you? Bossing me around, ruining my day?

BEN, *softly:* Be nice to the girl. You hear me?

OSCAR: I'm taking her home. That's enough. Damned little ninny.

BEN: I was thinking of trying to do you a favor. I was thinking if something works right for me, I'd lend you the five hundred to pay Papa back.

OSCAR: Squee, Ben! If you only could. What would you be doing it for?

BEN: Because I want you to be nice to this girl. Flatter her, talk nice. She's kind of pretty.

OSCAR: Pretty? I can't stand 'em like that.

BEN: I know. Virtue in woman offends you. Now go on. Be charming. Five hundred possible dollars' charming.

OSCAR, *smiles:* All right. *He runs off. After a minute Marcus, carrying three books and a bottle of wine, appears on the porch.*

MARCUS, *reading:* "The customary branches of education number four. Reading and writing." You know *those*, Benjamin, I think. "Gymnastic exercise"—*Marcus laughs*—"and music." Aristotle. *You* don't know any music, Benjamin.

BEN: I've been too busy, Papa.

MARCUS: At what?

BEN: Working all my life for you. Doing a lot of dirty jobs. And then watching you have a wild time throwing the money around. But when I ask you to lend me a little . . .

MARCUS: You're a free man, Benjamin. A free man. You don't like what I do, you don't stay with me. *Holding up the book:* I do wish you would read a little Aristotle, take your mind off money.

Regina comes down the steps, in a new dress, carrying a parasol and a steamer rug.

BEN, *looks at her:* Oh. Before I forget. I invited Miss Birdie Bagtry and her cousin to come here tomorrow night.

MARCUS: To come here? What do you mean?

BEN: I thought you'd like having the quality folk here. *Smiles:* Come here to beg a favor of you.

MARCUS, *stares at him, giggles:* You teasing me?

BEN: No. The girl just left here. She wants us to lend money on the cotton. Her Mama didn't know, and mustn't know. But Miss Birdie doesn't own the place—

MARCUS: Then what kind of nonsense is that?

BEN: Maybe it's not nonsense. Take a note from her. If she dies before her mother—

MARCUS, *sharply:* Who said anything about dying? You're very concerned with people dying, aren't you?

BEN, *laughs:* You hate that word. *Quickly:* Her mother could get out of it legally, maybe, but I don't think she would. Anyway, the old lady is sick, and it's worth a chance. Make it a short loan, call it in in a few years. They've wrecked the place and the money won't do 'em much good. I think the time would come when you'd own the plantation for almost nothing— *Looks up at Regina.* A loan would make them happy, and make us money. Make the Bagtrys grateful to us—

REGINA, *softly:* Course I don't know anything about business, Papa, but could I say something, please? I've been kind of lonely here with nobody nice having much to do with us. I'd sort of like to know people of my own age, a girl my own age, I mean—

MARCUS, *to Ben:* How much does she want?

BEN, *hesitates for a minute:* Ten thousand.

MARCUS: On Lionnet? Ten thousand is cheap. She's a fool.

BEN, *smiles:* Yes, I think she's a fool.

MARCUS, *giggles:* Well, the one thing I never doubted was your making a good business deal. Kind of cute of you to think of their coming here to get it, too. Bagtrys in this house, begging. Might be amusing for an hour.

REGINA, *quickly:* Can't invite 'em for an hour, Papa. And we've got to be nice to them. Otherwise I just wouldn't want to see him come unless we'd be awful nice and polite.

MARCUS: They'll think we're nice and polite for ten thousand.

REGINA, *laughs, in a high good humor:* I guess. But you be pleasant to them—

MARCUS: Why, Regina? Why are you so anxious?

REGINA: Papa, I told you. I been a little lonesome. No people my age ever coming here— I do think people like that sort of want to forgive you, and be nice to us—

MARCUS, *sharply, angrily:* Forgive me?

REGINA, *turns away, little-girl tearful:* I'm mighty sorry. What have I done? Just said I'd like to have a few people to listen to your old music. Is that so awful to want?

MARCUS, *quickly, pleadingly:* Come on, darling. *Shouts:* Lavinia, *where* is the basket? Lavinia! Coralee! *To Regina:* Come on now, honey. It's been a long time since you been willing to spend a Sunday with me. If I was sharp, I'm sorry. Don't you worry. I'll be charming to the visiting gentry.

BEN: Miss Birdie got a fear of asking you for the loan and of her cousin, John, knowing about it. Might be better if you just gave your consent, Papa, and didn't make her tell the story all over again. I can do the details.

Lavinia appears with a basket. Marcus takes it from her, peers in it.

MARCUS, *to Regina:* That's mighty nice-looking. We'll have a good lunch. *To Ben:* I don't want to hear the woes of Lionnet and Mistress Birdie. Most certainly you will do the details. Be kind of pleasant owning Lionnet. It's a beautiful house. Very light in motive, very well conceived—

LAVINIA: You going now, Marcus? Marcus! You promised you'd talk to me. Today—

MARCUS: I'm talking to you, Lavinia.

LAVINIA: Last year this morning, you promised me it would be today—

MARCUS, *gently:* I'm going out now, Lavinia.

LAVINIA: I've fixed you a mighty nice lunch, Marcus, the way you like it. I boiled up some crabs right fast, and—

MARCUS: I'm sure. Thank you. *He starts to move off.*

LAVINIA, *comes running to him:* Please, Marcus, I won't take up five minutes. Or when you come back? When you come back, Marcus?

MARCUS: Another day, my dear.

LAVINIA: It can't be another day, Marcus. It was to be on my birthday, this year. When you sat right in that chair, and I brought my Bible and you swore—

MARCUS: Another day.

LAVINIA: It ought to be today. If you swear to a day, it's got to be that day— *Very frightened:* Tomorrow then. Tomorrow wouldn't hurt so much, because to-morrow is just after today— I've *got* to go this week, because I had a letter from the Reverend—

REGINA: Oh, Mama. Are you talking that way again?

LAVINIA, *shaking, wildly:* Tomorrow, Marcus? Tomorrow, tomorrow.

MARCUS, *to Ben:* Ben, get Coralee.

LAVINIA: Tomorrow— *Ben exits. She grabs Marcus's arm:* Promise me tomorrow, Marcus. Promise me. I'll go get my Bible and you promise me—

MARCUS, *very sharply:* Stop that nonsense. Get hold of yourself. I've had enough of that! I want no more.

LAVINIA, *crying:* I'm not making any trouble. You know that, Marcus. Just promise me tomorrow.

MARCUS: Stop it! I've had enough. Try to act like you're not crazy. Get yourself in hand. *He exits.*

REGINA, *as Coralee appears:* Never mind, Mama. Maybe you'll be coming away with me. Would you like that? There are lots of churches in Chicago—

CORALEE: All right, Miss Regina. Don't tease her now.

REGINA, *gaily, as she goes off:* I'm not teasing.

After a pause, Lavinia sits down.

LAVINIA: Now I'm going to pretend. You ready?

CORALEE, *as if this had happened a thousand times before:* All right.

LAVINIA: He didn't say any of those things. He said he would speak with me sure thing— *Her voice rises:* No man breaks a Bible promise, and you can't tell me they do. You know I got my correspondence with the Reverend. He wants me to come and I got my mission and my carfare. In his last letter, the Reverend said if I was coming I should come, or should write him and say I couldn't ever come. "Couldn't ever come—" Why did he write that?

CORALEE: I don't know.

LAVINIA: Your people are my people. I got to do a little humble service. I lived in sin these thirty-seven years, Coralee. *Rocks herself.* Such sin I couldn't even tell you.

CORALEE: You told me.

LAVINIA: Now I got to finish with the sin. Now I got to do my mission. And I'll be— I'll do it nice, you know I will. I'll gather the little black children round, and I'll teach them good things. I'll teach them how to read and write, and sing the music notes and—

CORALEE, *wearily:* Oh, Miss Viney. Maybe it's just as well. Maybe they'd be scared of a white teacher coming among them.

LAVINIA, *after a pause:* Scared of me?

CORALEE, *turns:* No, ma'am. You're right. News of you has gone ahead.

LAVINIA: Course they could have many a better teacher.

I know mighty little, but I'm going to try to remember better. *Quietly:* And the first thing I'm going to remember is to speak to Marcus tomorrow. Tomorrow. *Turns pleadingly to Coralee:* I was silly to speak today. And I did it wrong. Anyway, he didn't say I *couldn't* go, he just said— *Stops suddenly.* My goodness, it's such a little thing to want. Just to go back where you were born and help little colored children to grow up knowing how to read books and— *Giggles.* You'll be proud of me. I'll remember things to teach them. You remember things when you're happy. And I'm going to be happy. You get to be fifty-nine, you don't be happy then, well, you got to find it. I'm going to be a very happy, happy, happy, happy— I'm going, Coralee. *She suddenly stops, looks down in her lap.*

CORALEE: Nice and cool in your room. Want to lie down? *Lavinia doesn't answer.* Want to play a little on the piano? Nobody's inside. *No answer. She waits, then very gently:* All right, if you don't want to. I tell you what. Come on in the kitchen and rest yourself with us.

Lavinia gets up, Coralee takes her arm, they start out as

CURTAIN FALLS

ACT TWO

SCENE: *The living room of the Hubbard house. This is the room we have seen through the French doors of the first act, and now we are looking at the room as if we were standing in the French doors of the portico. A large bay window is center stage, leading to a porch that faces the first-act portico. Right stage is a door leading to the dining room. Left stage is an open arch leading to the entrance hall and main staircase. The furniture is from the previous owner but Marcus has cleared the room of the ornaments and the ornamented. Right stage is a round table and three chairs. Left stage is a sofa and chair. Right, upstage, is a desk. Left, upstage, is a piano. Right, upstage, is a long table. Center of the room, before the columns of the porch, are a table and chairs. The room is simpler, more severe, than many rooms of the 1880's. A Greek vase, glass-enclosed, stands on a pedestal; a Greek statue sits on the table; Greek battle scenes are hung on the walls.*

As the curtain rises, Ben and Oscar are sitting at table, stage right. They each have a glass of port and the port decanter is in front of them. Marcus, Penniman and

44

*Jugger are standing at a music stand, looking down at
a music score. Penniman is a tall, fattish man. Jugger
looks like everybody. Penniman looks up from the score,
hums, drains his glass, looks at the empty glass, and
crosses to Ben and Oscar. Marcus is intent on the score.*

PENNIMAN, *meaning the score:* Very interesting. Har-
monically fresh, eh, Mr. Benjamin?

BEN: I know nothing of music.

JUGGER: Why do people always sound so proud when
they announce they know nothing of music?

PENNIMAN, *quickly, as Oscar fills his glass:* A fine port,
and a mighty good supper. I always look forward to our
evening here. I tell my wife Mrs. Hubbard is a rare
housekeeper.

BEN: You like good port, Mr. Penniman?

PENNIMAN: Yes, sir, and don't trust the man who don't.

*Oscar goes off into gales of laughter. This pleases Mr.
Penniman and he claps Oscar on the shoulder. Marcus
looks up, annoyed, taps bow on music stand. Penniman
and Oscar stop laughing, Penniman winks at Oscar,
carries his glass back to music stand. Jake comes from
the hall entrance carrying two chairs, a lamp, and passes
through to porch. Lavinia hurries in from the dining
room. Her hair is mussy, her dress spotted. She looks
around the room, smiles at everybody. When nobody
notices her, she crosses to Marcus, leans over to examine
the score, nods at what she reads.*

LAVINIA: Oh, it's nice, Marcus. Just as nice as anybody could have. It's going to be a cold collation. Is that all right?

MARCUS, *who is in a good humor:* Yes, certainly. What's that?

LAVINIA: A cold collation? That's what you call food when you have guests. A cold collation.

PENNIMAN, *looks toward the dining room, delighted:* More food? After that fine supper—

LAVINIA: This is a special night. Guests. Isn't that pleasant? My, we haven't had guests— I don't think I remember the last time we had guests—

MARCUS, *looks at her:* All right, Lavinia.

LAVINIA: There'll be a dish of crabs, of course. And a dish of crawfish boiled in white wine, the way Belle does. And a chicken salad, and a fine strong ham we've been saving. *Stops.* Oh. I'm worrying you gentlemen—

PENNIMAN, *lifting his glass:* Worrying us? You, the honor of Rose County, and the redeemer of this family—

Jugger and Marcus look up sharply. Ben laughs. Marcus reaches over and takes Penniman's glass, carries it to table.

MARCUS: I am awaiting your opinion.

PENNIMAN, *who has the quick dignity of a man with too much port:* The judgment of music, like the inspiration for it, must come slow and measured, if it comes with truth.

OSCAR, *to Ben:* Talks like a Christmas tree, don't he?

LAVINIA: It's your third composition, isn't it, Marcus? Oh, I'm sure it's lovely. Just lovely.

MARCUS, *looks at her—softly:* How would you know, Lavinia?

LAVINIA, *hurt:* I can read notes, Marcus. Why, I taught you how to read music. Don't you remember, Marcus? *She goes toward Ben and Oscar.* I did. Yes, I did.

BEN, *amused:* Of course you did.

PENNIMAN, *hurriedly:* I would say this: It is done as the Greeks might have imposed the violin upon the lute. *Hums.* Right here. Close to Buxtehude— *Inspiration:* Or, the Netherland Contrapuntalists. Excellent.

Oscar pours himself another port, Lavinia has wandered to the piano, mumbling to herself.

MARCUS, *very pleased, to Penniman:* You like it?

PENNIMAN: I like it very much. And if you would allow us, I would like to introduce it in Mobile during the season. Play it first at the school, say, then, *possibly—*

MARCUS: That would make me very happy. And what do you think of it, Mr. Jugger?

JUGGER, *slowly:* Penniman speaks for me. He always does.

PENNIMAN, *quickly:* Come. We'll try it for you. I am

most anxious to hear it. *Points to Marcus's violin, coyly:* I daresay you know the solo part you have written for yourself?

MARCUS: Well, I—yes. *Very pleased:* I had hoped you would want to try it tonight. I— *Jugger picks up his violin, starts for portico. Marcus turns to him:* Mr. Jugger. Would *you* like to try it now?

JUGGER, *turns, looks at Marcus, seems about to say something, changes his mind:* I would like to try.

PENNIMAN: But where *is* my cello? Goodness God—

JUGGER, *sharply, at door of portico:* It's out here. When will you learn that it's hard to mislay a cello? *Penniman giggles, trips out to porch.*

LAVINIA, *suddenly plays a few notes on the piano:* See? I told you, Marcus. *That's* it. I told you I could read music just as good as I used to—

MARCUS: Is there something disturbing you this evening, Lavinia? More than usual?

Regina enters from the hall. She is dressed up, very handsome. They all turn to stare at her. She smiles, goes to Marcus.

MARCUS, *softly:* You're a beautiful girl.

OSCAR: Looks like the decorated pig at the county fair.

REGINA, *wheels around for Marcus:* It's my Chicago dress. *One* of my Chicago dresses. *Regina notices Lavinia:* Oh, Mama, it's late. Do go and get dressed.

LAVINIA: I'm dressed, Regina.

REGINA: You can't look like that. Put on a nice silk—

LAVINIA: I only have what I have—

REGINA: Put on your nice dress, Mama. It will do for tonight. We must order you new things. You can't go to Chicago looking like a tired old country lady—

LAVINIA, *wheels around: Chicago?* I'm not going to Chicago. Where I'm going I don't need clothes or things of the world. I'm going to the poor, and it wouldn't be proper to parade in silk— Marcus! You tell Regina where I'm going. *Tell her where I'm going.* You tell her right now. You—

REGINA: All right, Mama. Now don't you fret. Go upstairs and get dressed up for the high-toned guests. *She leads Lavinia to the hall.* Don't you worry now. Go on up, honey. Coralee's waiting for you. *She comes back into room. To Marcus:* Whew! I'm sorry. I should have known. I hope she isn't going to act queer the rest of the evening.

MARCUS: There's always that chance.

REGINA: Well, don't let's worry. *Gaily:* I'll see to everything. I'd better have a look in the kitchen, and more chairs— Let's have the very good champagne, Papa?

PENNIMAN, *from portico:* Mr. Hubbard—

MARCUS, *takes keys from his pocket, throws them to Ben:* Wine as good as Regina's dress. And count the bottles used. I don't want to find that Oscar has sold them again.

BEN, *to Regina:* So your picnic was successful? When do you leave for Chicago?

REGINA, *gaily:* In ten days, two weeks. *Comes to him.* Going to miss me?

BEN: Yes. Very much.

MARCUS: What's the matter? What's the matter, Regina?

REGINA, *gaily, leaving Ben:* Matter? Nothing. *Calls into dining room as she exits:* Two more chairs, Jake—

OSCAR: Now just tell me how I'm going to get word to Laurette that I can't meet her till later tonight, just somebody tell me that.

MARCUS, *very sharply to Ben:* I told you to get the wine.

Ben looks at him, smiles as if he understood why Marcus was angry, exits through dining-room door. Marcus stands staring at him. Then goes to piano, looks through scores. Oscar moves nervously toward Marcus.

OSCAR, *desperately:* Papa, I'm in trouble. You see, I had an appointment with a lady from out of town, Roseville, I mean.

MARCUS: What were they doing?

OSCAR: Who?

MARCUS: Regina and Ben when they were standing together— *Breaks off, turns sharply away.*

OSCAR: Oh, you know Ben. Always up to something. Yesterday, trying to marry off Regina, tonight trying to press me on the Bagtry girl.

MARCUS, *looks up:* Oh, come. Ben's not a fool. You and a Bagtry is a very comic idea.

OSCAR: I know, but Ben's figured they're so hard up for money they might even have me. It all fits in with this mortgage you're giving them, or something. He's got his eye on the cotton— *Giggles.* And Ben's eye goes in a lot of directions, mostly around corners. It's true, Papa. He made me take the girl home yesterday—

MARCUS, *looks at Oscar:* The mortgage, and then the girl and you. Interesting man, Benjamin.

OSCAR, *pleadingly:* Papa, like I say. I've got a friend who's waiting for me right now. I want you to meet her. You see, I'm deeply and sincerely in love. Deeply and sincerely. She's a fine girl. But *Ben* cries her down. *Ben* don't want me to be happy.

MARCUS: Isn't that too bad. Your own brother. It's a shame.

OSCAR: Course she's of the lower classes, and that doesn't fit in with Ben's plans for us to marry money for him. But the lower classes don't matter to me; I always say it's not how people were born but what they are—

MARCUS: You always say that, eh? Well, some people are democrats by choice, and some by necessity. You, by necessity.

OSCAR: Could I go fetch her here—*Desperately:* to-night? Could I, Papa?

MARCUS: What is this, a night at the circus?

OSCAR, *slyly, as a last chance:* I think it would just about finish Mr. Ben to have a member of the lower classes, sort of, mixing with the gentry, here. I thought it would sort of, sort of amuse you, and well, you could meet her at the same time. Be a good joke on Ben, sort of—

MARCUS, *slowly:* Is this Laurette that, that little, er— little thing from Roseville you been steaming about?

OSCAR: She's not, Papa. Oh, maybe she was a little wild before I met her, but— She was left an orphan and she didn't know what else to do, starving and cold, friendless.

MARCUS, *shudders:* Oh God, shut up. *Hesitates, then laughs.* All right, go and get her, if you like. Er. Does she come dressed? I wouldn't like her here, er, unrobed.

OSCAR, *hurt but happy:* Aw, she's a fine woman, Papa, don't talk like that. And she loves music. She wants to learn just about everything—

MARCUS: Don't bring her as a student, Oscar.

OSCAR: Oh, no. No, I wouldn't. She won't say a word. She admires you, Papa—

MARCUS: For what?

OSCAR: Well, just about, well, just for everything, I guess— *Marcus makes a dismissive gesture, goes on porch as Regina comes into room. Oscar sees Regina, smiles.* I'll be back in a few minutes. Going across the square to get Laurette, bring her here.

REGINA, *starts toward him, as Ben comes in carrying champagne bottles:* Here? That girl?—What's the matter with you? You're doing nothing of the kind. Come back here. You can't bring that—

OSCAR: Can't I? Well, just ask Papa. *He* wants her to meet my folks.

REGINA, *turns to Ben:* Ben, stop him. He can't bring her here tonight— Stop him! *But Oscar has disappeared:* Get him, Ben!

BEN: What am I supposed to do, shoot him? I'm too old to run down streets after men in love.

REGINA: He *can't* bring her here. You know what John will think. I saw him this afternoon: I had to beg him to come tonight. He doesn't know why Birdie wants him to come, but— Ben, he'll think we meant to do it, planned to insult them—

BEN: Yes, I'm sure he will.

The music on the porch begins.

REGINA: What's the matter with Papa? Why did he let Oscar—

BEN, *smiles:* *You're* going to learn some day about Papa. It's not as easy as you think, Regina. *They stand looking out to the porch, listening to the music.* He gave those clowns five thousand last month for something they call their music school. Now that they are playing his composition he should be good for another five thousand—

REGINA, *turns, softly, amazed:* Did he? Really? *Shakes her head:* Well, anyway, he's promised me plenty for—

BEN: To marry Bagtry? Enough to support you the rest of your life, you and your husband? I'm taking a vacation the day he finds out about your marriage plans.

REGINA, *angrily, nervous:* I don't know what you're talking about. Marry— What are you saying—? I— *Turns to him, tensely:* Leave me alone, Ben. Leave me alone. Stop making trouble. If you dare say *anything* to Papa about John, I'll—

BEN, *very sharply:* Don't threaten me. I'm sick of threats.

REGINA, *angry:* You'll be much sicker of them if you— *Then, softly:* Ben, don't. I'm in love with John.

BEN, *softly:* But he's not in love with you.

Lavinia comes into room, followed by Coralee who is pulling at her, trying to button her dress. Regina turns away from Ben.

LAVINIA: Don't bother with the lower buttons. *Timidly:* Am I proper now, daughter? *Regina doesn't answer her. Lavinia points out to porch, meaning the music.* You know, I've made myself cheer up. I know you were just teasing about Chicago, Regina, and I know full well

I've never been good about teasing. What do people do now, curtsy or shake hands? I guess it's just about the first guests we had since the suspicion on your Papa.

REGINA: Now, Mama. Please don't talk about any of that tonight. Don't talk at all about the war, or anything that happened. Please remember, Mama. Do you hear?

CORALEE, *quickly:* She won't. You all have been teasing her, and she's tired.

Coralee goes to Ben, takes the champagne bottles from the table. Jake comes in from the dining room carrying a tray of glasses and a punch bowl.

LAVINIA: Could I try the nice punch, Coralee?

CORALEE: You certainly can. *Jake exits. Ben starts to the table. As if such courtesy were unusual, Coralee stares at him:* Thank you, Mr. Ben.

Coralee exits. Ben pours three glasses of punch.

LAVINIA: Regina, when you don't frown you look like my Grandmama—*as Ben brings her a glass of punch, and moves on to Regina*—the one who taught me to read and write. And 'twas mighty unusual, a lady to know how to read and write, up in the piney woods.

BEN, *laughs:* Now, that's a safer subject, Mama. Tell the Bagtrys about our kinfolk in the piney woods. *He lifts his glass to Regina.* To you, honey.

REGINA, *smiles:* And to you, *honey.*

On the porch the music comes to an end. Regina who

has not, of course, been paying any attention, starts to
applaud. She turns to Lavinia, indicates Marcus on
porch.

LAVINIA: But I didn't hear it. I wasn't paying any attention.

Marcus comes into room.

REGINA, *goes to him:* It's brilliant of you, Papa.

MARCUS: I'm glad you liked it. Come along. We're about
to start—*laughs*—the better-known classics.

BEN: Won't you wait for our guests?

MARCUS: Certainly not. I resent their thinking they can
stroll in late on my music.

REGINA, *placatingly:* You're right, darling. *We'll* come
out.

Marcus goes to porch. Regina follows. Ben follows her.
Lavinia puts down her glass, follows Ben. Regina and
Ben sit down, Lavinia sits down. The musicians tune
up. Marcus, Penniman, and Jugger begin to play a di-
vertimento by Leopold Mozart, a trio for violin, viola,
and cello. Then the hall door opens and closes. On the
porch, Regina and Ben both turn, turn back again.
After a second, Oscar appears in the living room pull-
ing Laurette Sincee. Laurette is about twenty, pig-face
cute, a little too fashionably dressed. She stands in the
door, admiring the room.

LAURETTE: Squee!

OSCAR, *proud and excited:* Not bad, eh? *Looks toward*
portico. We got to talk soft.

LAURETTE: This *is* nice. You born here, Oskie?

OSCAR: No. Like I told you. Right after the war Papa bought—*giggles*—or something, this house from old man Reed. Like it?

LAURETTE: Squee. Who wouldn't?

OSCAR: Well, maybe, some day—

LAURETTE: Ah, go on, Oskie. **Go on.**

OSCAR: You just wait and see.

LAURETTE, *points to portico:* What's that?

OSCAR: What?

LAURETTE: The noise?

OSCAR: That's music, honey.

LAURETTE: Oh.

OSCAR: When you speak to Papa, tell him how much you like music. Tell him how fine he plays.

LAURETTE: What's he playing?

OSCAR: The violin.

LAURETTE: Ain't that a coincidence? I had a beau who said he played the violin. A Frenchman, much older than me. Had to leave his very own country because of the revolution.

OSCAR, *winces:* I don't like to hear about him, Laurette, him or any other men. I am deeply and sincerely in love with you.

LAURETTE, *pleasantly, but without too much interest:* Are you really, Oskie?

OSCAR: Laurette, I'm going to ask Papa for a loan. Then we'll go on down to New Orleans. Would you, Laurette—

LAURETTE: You've asked me the same question for the last year, twenty times. But you never yet asked your Papa for the loan.

OSCAR: I've been waiting for the right opportunity. I want you to be my *wife,* honey. I am deeply and—

LAURETTE: We can't eat on deeply and sincerely.

OSCAR: No, I know. But this is the big night, don't you see? *Laughs happily.* I never thought he'd let you come here. I mean—I mean a chance like this. And he's in a good humor about something. Now, darling, be very very—well, er. I tell you: you speak with him about what *he* likes. Tell him how much you think of music, not new music, mind you, but—and tell him how you stay awake reading.

LAURETTE: I've always been a reader. But I can't talk about it. What's there to say?

OSCAR: And he's fond of Mozart. Talk about Mozart.

LAURETTE: I can't do that.

OSCAR: Well, just try to please him. So much depends on it. We could have our own little place in New Orleans—

LAURETTE: What kind of place?

OSCAR: I'd find a job. You bet I would, and with you behind me to encourage and love me, with you to fight for, I'd forge ahead.

LAURETTE, *looks at him, puzzled:* Oh. Well, I'd certainly like to go to New Orleans. I know a girl there. She has an embroidery shop on Royal Street. I'm good at embroidery. It's what I always wanted to do. Did I ever tell you that? Always wanted to do embroidery. ·

OSCAR: Did you?

LAURETTE: Yep. Instead of whoring. I just wanted to do fancy embroidery.

OSCAR, *loudly, in a hurt cry:* Don't, Laurette, don't talk that way! *Ben and Regina, on the porch, look into room. Regina coughs loudly.* We better go out now.

LAURETTE: Why did your papa let me come tonight?

OSCAR: Don't let him worry you, honey. Just take it nice and easy. Pretend nobody knows anything about you, pretend you're just as good as them—

LAURETTE, *stares at him: Pretend?* Pretend I'm as good as anybody called Hubbard? Why, my Pa died at Vicksburg. He didn't stay home bleeding the whole state of Alabama with money tricks, and suspected of worse. You think I been worried for that reason?

OSCAR, *desperately:* No, no. I— For God's sake don't talk like that—

LAURETTE: You may be the rich of this county, but everybody knows how. Why, the Frenchman, I used to eat dinner with, and his sister, the Countess. What you mean, boy, your folks—?

OSCAR: I didn't mean anything bad. Haven't I just said I wanted to *marry* you? I think you're better than anybody.

LAURETTE: I'm not better than anybody, but I'm as good as piney wood crooks.

OSCAR, *puts his hand over her mouth, looks toward porch:* Stop, *please.* We've got to go outside. *Please—*

LAURETTE, *good-natured again:* Sometimes you bring out the worst in my nature, Oskie, and make me talk foolish. Squee, it's the truth—I am a little twitchy about coming here and meeting your folks. That's why I'm talking so brave. I ain't been in a place like this before. . . . *Pats him:* All right, I'll be very good and nice. I would like to go to New Orleans.

Oscar takes her in his arms. The front bell rings, but they don't hear it.

OSCAR: Course you would, with me. You love me, honey? *He leans down to kiss her.* Tell me you love me.

LAURETTE: Now, Oskie, you know this ain't the place or the time for mush—

Ben rises at the sound of the bell. As Ben comes from the porch, Jake brings in the Bagtrys. As they enter, Oscar is kissing Laurette, she is giggling, trying to push him away. The Bagtrys stop in the doorway as they see the scene. Ben comes to meet them, crosses stage. As he passes Oscar and Laurette, he shoves Oscar.

BEN: Excuse me. *As Laurette jumps away, Regina comes in from porch, tapping Lavinia on the arm as she comes. Ben speaks to Birdie:* My apologies. We don't always arrange this scene for our guests.

Birdie smiles nervously. John stares at Laurette.

OSCAR: We were just, I was, we were—

REGINA, *sharply:* All right. *Goes quickly to Birdie:* I am happy to have you here, Miss Birdie.

Birdie curtsies, puts out her hand, smiles warmly. Lavinia enters room.

JOHN, *bows to Regina, Ben, Oscar, then speaks to Laurette:* Hello, Laurette.

LAURETTE: Hello, John.

JOHN, *turns to Birdie:* Birdie, this is Miss Sincee.

LAURETTE: Finely, thank you.

Birdie bows.

LAVINIA, *hears Laurette speak and so hurries to her:* An honor to have you here, Miss Birdie—

REGINA, *sharply:*   This is Miss Birdie, Mama.

LAVINIA, *who is shaking hands with Laurette, looks bewildered:* Oh. Sorry. I—

Oscar bumps into Lavinia, who is coming toward Birdie.

BIRDIE: I'm sorry we're late. I just couldn't seem to get dressed—

REGINA: Do come out now for the music.

They move out together. Lavinia speaks to Birdie.

LAVINIA: Come, ma'am. And you, Miss— *Brightly, to Birdie:* Is the other lady your sister?

LAURETTE, *annoyed, shoves Oscar:* What's the matter with you?

OSCAR: Oh. Mama, this is Miss Laurette Sincee. She's a visitor in town.

LAVINIA: Who's she visiting?

BEN: Us.

Ben reaches the porch door, stands aside to let Lavinia pass him. She looks puzzled, passes on to porch. Laurette, Oscar, Regina, John, are now seated on the porch. Lavinia sits near them. Birdie and Ben stand for a minute listening to the music.

BIRDIE: Nice. To have a special night, just to play music— I've heard your father is a very cultured gentleman. Have you been able, did he, speak of the matter that I—

BEN: Yes. We will make the loan.

BIRDIE, *turns radiant—softly:* Oh, what fine news! You can't imagine how worried I've been. I am very grateful to you, sir—

BEN: You don't have to be. It is a good loan for Hubbard Company, or my father wouldn't be taking it. We'll meet tomorrow, you and I, and work out the details.

BIRDIE: Oh, you won't have any trouble with me, Mr. Ben.

BEN: You wanted five thousand dollars, Miss Birdie. I have asked my father to lend you ten thousand.

BIRDIE, *puzzled—worried:* Oh. Mr. Ben, I don't need—

BEN, *quickly:* You can take five now, but if you should happen to need more, it will be there for you.

BIRDIE: But I won't need ten thousand dollars. No, indeed I won't. It's very kind of you, but—

BEN, *carefully:* You will only get five. I will keep the rest waiting for you. That's the way these things are done—*smiles*—sometimes.

BIRDIE: But it's bad enough to owe five thousand, not less ten—

BEN: *You will only owe five.* Now don't worry about it. Will you take my advice now about something else? Don't speak to my father about the loan. It is all arranged. And he's a man of such culture, as you say, that talk of money would disturb him on his music night.

BIRDIE, *gently:* Oh, of course. After all, it's a party, and as worried and pushing as I am, I wouldn't ever have talked business with him at a party.

BEN, *smiles down at her:* Good breeding is very useful. Thank you, Miss Birdie.

BIRDIE, *gently:* No, sir. It is I who must thank you.

He bows, stands aside, indicates porch. She moves to it, sits down. Ben stands in the doorway. The music continues. After a minute we see Oscar trying to move into the room. He leans over, bends down, moves rapidly into room, passes Ben. Laurette turns and Oscar beckons to her to come into room.

OSCAR: Papa going to play all night? *Crosses to get a drink.* Laurette's getting restless, sitting there.

BEN: She's not accustomed to a sitting position? Have another drink. I got a feeling you're going to need it.

LAURETTE, *enters the room from the porch:* Squee. I don't like this punch. It don't mean anything.

BEN: Can I put in a little brandy? I think that would make it mean more.

Marcus appears on the porch, comes up the aisle of chairs. He bows to Birdie and to John, comes into room. Oscar rushes to get him a drink of punch.

OSCAR: Papa, this is Miss Sincee.

MARCUS, *finishes drink, hands glass to Oscar:* How do you do?

LAURETTE: Finely, thank you. *Marcus stares at her. She becomes very nervous.* I love music, Mr. Hubbard. I had an uncle who played. *He* taught me to love music.

OSCAR, *too brightly:* Did he play the violin, like Papa?

LAURETTE: Er. Er. No. He had a little drum.

OSCAR, *very fast:* He liked Mozart. You told me, remember?

LAURETTE: Yeah. Sure did.

Regina and Birdie, followed by John and Lavinia, come in from the porch.

MARCUS: Miss Sincee pleases me. Her uncle played Mozart on a little drum. Have you ever heard of that, Miss Bagtry?

BIRDIE: Oh. Well, *I* haven't, but I'm sure there must be such an arrangement.

MARCUS, *looks at her with interest:* That's very kind of you, to be so sure. Do you play any instrument, Miss Bagtry? Not the little drum?

BIRDIE: Yes, sir. Not well. The piano.

MARCUS: Then you would oblige me—*she smiles, moves toward the piano, quickly*—some other night, very soon.

BIRDIE, *very flustered:* Yes. Yes, sir.

OSCAR: It's a coincidence, ain't it, that Laurette's Papa liked Mozart?

REGINA, *to Laurette:* I thought it was your uncle? Was your Papa the same as your uncle?

LAURETTE: What do you mean? Do you mean mon père was on one side of my family, and mon oncle on the other? I can understand *that*.

BEN, *fills her glass from the brandy decanter:* Your family were French?

LAURETTE: No. I learned that from a French gentleman who came from France. I don't know where he is now. I liked him.

BEN: Perhaps we could locate him for you.

LAURETTE: No. He married money.

REGINA: Oh, dear. All foreigners do, I guess. Light wines and light money.

LAURETTE: I never blamed him. I figured, well— *Looks at Regina:* You've had some bad experiences with Frenchmen?

Regina, Ben, and Marcus laugh.

BIRDIE, *to Marcus—making conversation:* John's been to Europe, you know.

MARCUS: I didn't know.

BIRDIE: Yes, he was. Just a few months before the war. Paris, France; London, England; St. Petersburg, Russia; Florence, Italy; Lake Como, Switzerland—

MARCUS: Your geography is remarkable.

BIRDIE: Oh, I only know because John kept a book. Pictures and notes and menus—if the war hadn't come, and my Papa had lived, I would have gone to Europe. It was planned for me to study water color.

MARCUS: Water color?

BIRDIE: Small water color. I like small water color.

MARCUS: Is that very different from large water color?

LAURETTE, *belligerently:* She means she likes small water color. What's the matter with that?

BIRDIE, *smiles at her:* Yes. *To Marcus:* You've been to Europe, Mr. Hubbard?

MARCUS, *laughs:* No, but I'm going. Might even settle down there. Yes, Regina?

REGINA, *looks at John, nervously:* Maybe some day, Papa. Chicago first.

MARCUS: Of course, we'll take our residence in Greece, but some place gayer, for Regina, at first. Perhaps you'd advise us, Captain Bagtry?

JOHN: I'd like to, sir. But I have no memory of Europe.

MARCUS, *turns elaborately in his chair:* Something unpleasant took it from your mind?

JOHN: No, sir. I just don't remember. It's as if I had never been there.

LAVINIA: I used to have a good memory. *Quickly:* I still have. Most of the time.

MARCUS, *very politely, to John:* Captain Bagtry, does anything stay in your memory, anything at all?

JOHN, *looks at Marcus, but the tone has been polite:* The war.

REGINA, *softly:* Only the war?

LAVINIA, *to John, motherly:* Well, I just bet. That's natural: you rode off so young.

JOHN, *turns to her:* Yes, ma'am. I can't remember the years before, and the years after have just passed like a wasted day. But the morning I rode off, and for three years, three months, and eight days after, well, I guess I remember every soldier, every gun, every meal, even every dream I had at night—

Ben is pouring Laurette another drink. Oscar is trying to keep her from having it. She pushes Oscar's hand.

LAURETTE: I wouldn't ever name a boy Oscar. It's silly.

REGINA: Well?

Marcus and Ben laugh. The others look embarrassed. Oscar makes an angry move, decides not to speak.

LAVINIA: I can't remember why we chose the name. Can you, Marcus?

MARCUS, *to Lavinia:* Your father's name was Oscar.

LAVINIA, *worried, crushed:* Oh, goodness, yes.

BIRDIE, *embarrassed, speaks quickly:* John's just wonderful about the war, Mr. Hubbard. Just as good as having a history book. He was everywhere: Vicksburg, Chattanooga, Atlanta.

MARCUS: And he remembers it *all?* What now seems to you the most important of your battles, Captain Bagtry?

JOHN, *annoyed:* I don't know. But there's no need for us to talk about the war, sir.

MARCUS: Oh, I'm interested. I know more of the Greek wars than I do of our own.

LAURETTE: Bet you anything there's a good reason for that. There's a good reason for everything in this vale of tears.

Marcus turns to stare at her.

BIRDIE: John, Mr. Hubbard says he's interested. Bet he'd like to hear about Vicksburg, just the way you always tell it to Mama and me.

Jake appears at the door.

JAKE: Supper's laid out, waiting.

MARCUS, *to John:* People remember what made them happy, and you were happy in the war, weren't you?

JOHN: Yes, sir. I was happy. I thought we would win.

MARCUS: I never did. Never, from the first foolish talk to the last foolish day. *John sharply turns away.* I have disturbed you. I'm most sorry. I speak the truth—whenever I can.

BIRDIE, *hastily:* Oh, John doesn't mind. He means— well, you see, it's hard for us to understand anybody who thought we'd lose—

JOHN, *sharply:* It's still hard for a soldier to understand.

BIRDIE, *quickly:* John means once a soldier, always a soldier. He wants to go to Brazil right now. Of course you know, Mr. Hubbard, the radical people down there are trying to abolish slavery, and ruin the country. John wants to fight for his ideals.

MARCUS: Why don't you choose the other side? Every man needs to win once in his life.

JOHN, *angrily:* I don't like that way of saying it. I don't necessarily fight for slavery, I fight for a way of life.

MARCUS: Supper, Captain. *Turns, calls to the porch:* Put away the music, gentlemen, and have a little more to eat. *Turns back to Regina:* What is disturbing you, Regina?

Lavinia, Birdie, Oscar, and Laurette exit to dining room.

REGINA, *sharply:* Nothing.

Ben exits.

MARCUS, *looks at John:* You disapprove of me, Captain?

JOHN: I am in your house, sir, and you forced me into this kind of talk.

Penniman and Jugger come through the room, go into the dining room.

MARCUS: Well, I disapprove of you. Your people deserved to lose their war and their world. It was a backward world, getting in the way of history. Appalling that you still don't realize it. Really, people should read more books.

REGINA, *angrily:* Papa, I didn't ask John here to listen to you lecture and be nasty and insulting.

MARCUS: *You* asked him here? You asked *John?* *Sharply:* Come in to supper, Regina.

REGINA, *very sharply:* When I'm ready, Papa. *Marcus*

looks at her, hesitates for a second, then goes into dining room. There is a pause. She goes to John: I am so sorry.

JOHN: Why should you be sorry? It's the way you feel, too.

REGINA, *impatiently:* All that damn war nonsense— Don't worry about Papa. I'll take care of him. You didn't give me a chance to tell you about Chicago—

JOHN: You didn't give me a chance to tell you about Brazil.

REGINA: Will you stop that foolish joke—

JOHN: It may not be a joke. Birdie has a plan. She won't tell me about it. Anyway, she says there's going to be money to run Lionnet and enough for me to borrow a little. I'll go on down to Brazil right away. Cod Carter says there's no trick in getting a commission with good pay. The planters there are looking for Confederate officers. I want to be with fighting men again. I'm lonely for them.

REGINA: Now you stop frightening me. I'm going to Chicago, and a month later you're coming and we'll get married. When Papa finds out he'll have a fit. Then we'll come on home for a while, and I'll talk him out of his fit—

JOHN, *gently, smiles:* Now you're joking. Don't talk silly, honey.

REGINA, *softly:* You don't want to come with me? You don't want to marry me?

JOHN, *after a second:* You don't ask that seriously.

REGINA, *softly:* Answer me, please.

JOHN: No. I don't. I never said I did. *Comes to her.* I don't want to talk this way, but I don't want to lie, either. Honey, I like you so much, but—I shouldn't have let us get like this. You're not in love with me. I'm no good for you—

REGINA: I am in love with you. I've never loved before, and I won't love again.

JOHN: My darling child, everybody thinks that, the first time. You're a lonely girl and I'm the first man you've liked. You can have anybody you want—

REGINA: John. Come away with me. We'll be alone. And after a while, if you still don't want me, then— *Softly:* I've never pleaded for anything in my life before. I might hold it against you.

JOHN: Oh, Regina, don't speak of pleading. You go away. By the time you come back, you'll be in love with somebody else, and I'll be gone.

REGINA, *stares at him:* Where did you say Miss Birdie was getting this money, this money for you to travel with?

JOHN: I don't know where: she won't tell me. But she says we'll have five thousand dollars this week.

REGINA, *after a second:* Five thousand?

JOHN, *nods:* I'd guess she's arranged something about

the Gilbert Stuart or the West. We haven't anything
but the portraits—

REGINA: Is that what you'd guess? Well, I'd guess different. So she's planning to get you away from me?

JOHN: Nobody's *planning* anything. Oh, look, honey.
This isn't any good. We'll go home now—

REGINA, *quickly, looking toward dining room:* Papa's
coming. Please go in to supper now. It will be bad for
me if you make any fuss or left now— *Softly:* We'll talk
tomorrow. I love you. Go in to supper.

Marcus appears in the dining-room door.

JOHN, *who has his back to the door:* I'm sorry, honey,
if— *He turns, moves across room, passes Marcus in the
doorway, disappears into the dining room.*

Marcus stares at Regina; she does not look at him.

MARCUS: Who is sillier, who is more dead, the captain
or his cousin? *She doesn't answer him.* You have a
reason for not joining us at supper?

REGINA: I wanted to talk to—to Captain Bagtry.

MARCUS: Can he talk of anything but war?

REGINA: Have you agreed to make Ben's loan on Lionnet?

MARCUS: Ben's loan? Of course I'll make it. It is good
for me, and bad for them. Got nothing to do with Ben.

REGINA: No? Have you asked yourself why Ben wants
it so much?

MARCUS: I am not interested in Ben's motives. As long as they benefit me, he is welcome to them.

REGINA: How much money did he say Miss Birdie had asked for?

MARCUS: Ten thousand. *Regina smiles.* Why does this interest you?

REGINA, *rises:* Don't make the loan, Papa. I don't like the girl. I think she's come here tonight to make fun of us. She's snubbing all of us, laughing up her sleeve. Why should you pay her to do it?

MARCUS, *stares at her:* That's not true and I don't think you think it is. You're lying to me about something. Stop it. It hurts me. Tell me why you were talking to that man, why he called you honey—

REGINA, *carefully:* Ben is sometimes smarter than you are, and you are so sure he isn't, that you get careless about him. *Nods toward dining room.* Bagtry doesn't know about *your* loan on Lionnet, but the girl told him she was getting five thousand dollars this week. *Five thousand dollars, not ten.* I'd like to bet the extra five is meant for Ben to keep. *Carefully, as he stares at her:* You're getting older, Papa, and maybe you're getting tired and don't think as fast. I guess that happens to everybody. You'll have to start watching Ben even more—

MARCUS, *sharply:* All right, Regina.

Penniman and Jugger come in from the dining room.

They stand awkwardly, not knowing what to do. Regina goes into dining room.

PENNIMAN, *hesitates:* Shall we—would you like us to continue the music?

MARCUS: As soon as you have finished overeating.

Penniman coughs, embarrassed. Jugger starts forward angrily, then stops, follows Penniman out to the porch. Lavinia comes in from the dining room.

LAVINIA: I think that Miss Laurette has a touch of heart trouble. I asked the poor child what she was doing for it. She said she was trying to see if good, strong drinks would help. I've never heard that, although Ben says it's a good cure. She's a nice little thing.

MARCUS: You've always been a good judge of people, Lavinia, but that's true of all the pure in heart, isn't it?

Laurette, followed by Oscar, comes into the room. She is steady, but the liquor has blinded her a little, and she bumps into things. Oscar follows her, very nervous, staring at Marcus, who does not turn around.

LAVINIA, *speaks to Laurette only because she is nervous:* Hello.

Laurette now finds herself near the piano. She strikes a note. Pleased, she presses her right hand on the keyboard. Delighted, she presses both hands. Oscar jumps toward her.

LAURETTE: Hello . . . I never had opportunities . . . *Oscar grabs both her hands, she pulls them away, pounds again, grins, indicates Marcus:* Your Papa likes music, he says.

MARCUS, *to Oscar:* Is there any effective way of stopping that?

Laurette throws off Oscar, comes over to Marcus.

LAURETTE: Oskie says he wants to marry little old Laurette.

MARCUS: Does little old Laurette think that fortunate?

LAURETTE, *laughs—puts her hand through his arm:* Sometimes yes, sometimes no. We're going on down to New Orleans.

Ben and Birdie come in from the dining room.

MARCUS, *takes Laurette's hand from his arm:* This will sound very rude but I have a nervous dislike of being grabbed.

LAURETTE: Oh, sure. Me, too. Can't stand people pressing me unless I know about it, I mean. *Glares at Oscar:* Don't you ever press me, Oskie, unless I know about it.

MARCUS: That reminds me. I'm told you work for a living. That is good: Oscar is not a rich man.

LAURETTE, *laughs:* Rich? How could he be, on that stinking slave salary you pay him? That's why you're sure to repent and help us, Oskie says. When you die you're going to leave it to him anyway, so why not now, Oskie says?

MARCUS, *softly:* Oscar is a liar. Always has been. *Birdie moves toward porch.* And he steals a little. Nothing much, not enough to be respectable. But you know all that, of course.

LAVINIA: Oh, Marcus. *Turns to Birdie:* My husband makes little jokes. All the time—

OSCAR, *very loudly, to Marcus:* It's not true. It's just not true—

MARCUS, *to Birdie:* Miss Bagtry, don't you find that people always think you're joking when you speak the truth in a soft voice?

BIRDIE, *very embarrassed:* No, sir. I—

MARCUS, *back to Laurette:* If you want him, Miss Laurette, do have him.

OSCAR, *with dignity:* Come on, Laurette. I'll settle this later.

Marcus laughs.

LAURETTE: Well, I'll just about say you will. A Papa talking about his son! No animal would talk about their own son that way. I heard tales about you ever since I was born, but—

OSCAR, *frantic:* Come on, Laurette.

LAURETTE: You old bastard.

Marcus slowly rises.

LAVINIA, *to Laurette:* Dear child—

LAURETTE, *to Marcus:* Everybody in this county knows how you got rich, bringing in salt and making poor, dying people give up everything for it. Right in the middle of the war, men dying for you, and you making their kinfolk give you all their goods and money—and I heard how they suspected you of worse, and you only just got out of a hanging rope. *Points to Oscar:* Why, the first night he slept with me, I didn't even want to speak to him because of you and your doings. My uncle used to tell me about—

BEN: Go on, Oscar. Get out.

John and Regina come in from dining room.

MARCUS, *to Oscar:* Take that girl out of here. Then come back. And come back quickly.

Oscar stares at him, starts to speak, changes his mind. Then he hurries to Laurette, takes her arm, moves her out. John crosses to Birdie.

LAVINIA, *in an odd tone:* Why, Marcus. The girl only told the truth. Salt is just a word, it's in the Bible quite a lot. And that other matter, why, death is also just a word. And—

MARCUS: You grow daring, Lavinia. *Moves toward her.* Now stop that prattling or go to your room—

BEN, *moves in front of him:* We have guests.

JOHN, *takes Birdie's arm, comes forward:* Good night and thank you, Mrs. Hubbard. *Coldly, to others:* Good night.

MARCUS: You came to beg a favor, and you stayed to be amused. Good night.

BIRDIE, *scared:* Mr. Hubbard, please . . .

JOHN: Came to ask a favor? From you? Who in this county would be so dishonored? If you were not an old man, Mr. Hubbard, I—

MARCUS: There is never so great a hero as the man who fought on a losing side.

BIRDIE, *goes to John—desperate:* Stop it, John. Go outside. Wait for me in the carriage.

JOHN: I don't want you here. Come on, Birdie—

BIRDIE, *firmly:* I want to stay for a few minutes. Please go outside. *Please. Please.*

He stares at her, then he turns, moves quickly out of the room. Marcus is watching Regina. Regina looks at Marcus, then turns and moves quickly after John. Marcus wheels around as if to stop Regina.

BIRDIE: Mr. Hubbard, I am sorry. John is upset. You know that his twin brother was killed that night in the massacre, and any mention of it—

MARCUS, *sharply:* What night do you speak of, Miss Birdie, and what massacre?

BIRDIE, *desperately:* Oh, I don't know. I—I'm just so sorry it has been unpleasant. I was hoping we could all be nice friends. Your family and mine—

MARCUS, *smiles:* Your mother hasn't bowed to me in the forty years I've lived in this town. Does she wish to be my nice friend now?

BIRDIE, *desperate:* Mama is old-fashioned. I'll speak to her and after a bit— *Pauses, looks down.* Oh. I've said the wrong thing again. I don't know how to— *Turns to him, simply:* I guess I just better say it simple, the way it comes to me. I didn't only come tonight for the loan. I *wanted* to come. I was frightened, of course, but, well, it was a big holiday for me, and I tried to get all dressed up in Mama's old things, and that was why we were late because I haven't had a new dress, and I've never had a party dress since I was four years old, and I had to get the dress without Mama's knowing why or where we were going, and I had to sew—

MARCUS: Then it *is* too bad you troubled yourself, because I have bad news for you: I have decided not to make the loan.

Birdie draws back, turns to Ben, starts to speak, puts her hands to her face.

BEN, *slowly:* Why? Why? You said yourself—

BIRDIE, *moves toward him:* Oh, please, Mr. Hubbard. Please. I went around all day telling our people they might be paid and—I'll give more, whatever you want—

MARCUS: That is unjust of you. I am not bargaining.

BEN, *angrily, to Marcus:* I want to know why you have changed your mind.

MARCUS: I will tell you, in time. *Turns to Birdie:* I am sorry to disappoint you. Please come another night, without a motive, just for the music.

BIRDIE: Yes, I had a motive. Why shouldn't I have? It was why I was asked here— Oh, I mustn't talk proud.

I have no right to. Look, Mr. Hubbard, I'll do anything. I'm sure you like good pictures: we have a Stuart and a West, and a little silver left. Couldn't I give— couldn't I bring them to you—

MARCUS, *gently, hurt:* Miss Birdie, Miss Birdie, please spare us both.

BIRDIE, *softly:* I was going to use the first money to buy molasses and sugar. All that land and cotton and we're starving. It sounds crazy, to need even molasses—

MARCUS: Everybody with cotton is starving.

BIRDIE, *angrily:* That's just a way of using a word. That isn't what I mean. I mean starving. *She looks up at him, her voice changes, sighs:* I should have known I couldn't do anything right. I never have. I'm sorry to have told you such things about us. You lose your manners when you're poor. *Goes to Lavinia:* Thank you, ma'am.

LAVINIA, *smiles gently, takes her hand:* Good night, child. You ride over and see me, or come down by the river and we'll read together.

BIRDIE, *smiles, crosses to Ben:* Thank you, Mr. Ben. I know you acted as my good friend.

MARCUS, *laughs:* Good night.

She nods, runs out.

LAVINIA, *after a second:* Goodness, Marcus. Couldn't you have—it's pig mean, being poor. Takes away your dignity.

MARCUS: That's correct, Lavinia. And a good reason for staying rich.

PENNIMAN'S VOICE: We're waiting for you, Mr. Hubbard.

MARCUS, *calling out:* That will be all for tonight.

Regina appears from the hall.

REGINA, *to Marcus:* I didn't intend you to insult them and make enemies of them.

MARCUS: Why are you so disturbed about the Bagtrys? *Ben laughs.* You are amused?

BEN: Yes. I am amused.

MARCUS: All right. Enjoy yourself—for a few minutes. *Penniman and Jugger appear carrying their instruments. Marcus turns to them:* The Mozart was carelessly performed. The carriage is waiting to take you to the station. Good night.

JUGGER: "Carelessly performed." What do you know about music? Nothing, and we're just here to pretend you do. Glad to make a little money once a month— *Angrily:* I won't do it any more, do you hear me?

MARCUS: Very well. Good night.

Jugger moves quickly out. Penniman comes forward, nervously.

PENNIMAN: He didn't mean—Gil is tired— Why, we're just as happy to come here— *No answer. Desperately:* Well, see you next month, sir. Just as usual. Huh?

When Marcus doesn't answer, Penniman sighs, exits as Oscar appears from porch.

OSCAR, *rushes toward Ben:* Trying to ruin my life, are you? Pouring liquor down her. Come on outside and fight it out like a man. I'll beat you up for it, the way you deserve—

LAVINIA, *as if she had come out of a doze:* Oh, goodness! The blood of brothers. *To Ben:* You in trouble, Ben? *Sees Oscar.* Oh, *you're* in trouble, Oscar.

OSCAR: Come on—

BEN: Oh, shut up.

Marcus laughs.

OSCAR, *turns on Marcus, angrily:* You laugh. I told you he had his eye on Birdie and Lionnet, and me getting it for him. So I fool him by bringing Laurette here. And then *he* fools *you:* gets Laurette drunk, and you get mad. That's just what he wanted you to do. And you did it for him. I think the joke's kind of on you.

REGINA: You must have told the truth once before in your life, Oscar, but I can't remember it.

MARCUS, *to Ben:* You're full of tricks these days. Did you get the girl drunk?

BEN: Just as good for Oscar to marry a silly girl who owns cotton, as a silly girl who doesn't even own the mattress on which she—

Oscar springs toward Ben, grabs his shoulder.

MARCUS, *to Oscar:* Will you stop running about and pulling at people? Go outside and shoot a passing nigger if your blood is throwing clots into your head.

OSCAR: I'm going to kill Ben if he doesn't stop—

MARCUS: Are you denying the girl makes use of a mattress, or do you expect to go through life killing every man who knows she does?

OSCAR, *screaming:* Papa, stop it! I am deeply and sincerely in love.

MARCUS: In one minute I shall put you out of the room. *Looks at Ben:* So that was the way it was supposed to work? Or better than that: the girl was to borrow ten thousand from me and you were to keep five of it, and take your chances on her being a fool, and nobody finding out.

BEN, *slowly:* I understand now. *Softly to Regina:* Bagtry told *you.* Yes? *Regina nods, smiles, sits down.*

MARCUS: Your tricks are getting nasty and they bore me. I don't like to be bored: I've told you that before.

BEN, *shrugs:* I want something for myself. I shouldn't think you were the man to blame me for that.

MARCUS: I wouldn't have, if you hadn't always been such a failure at getting it. *Goes to Ben:* I'm tired of your games, do you hear me? You're a clerk in my store and that you'll remain. You won't get the chance to try anything like this again. But in case you anger me once more, there won't be the job in the store, and you won't be here. Is that clear?

BEN, *slowly:* Very clear.

OSCAR, *who has been thinking:* Papa, you couldn't condemn a woman for a past that was filled with loathing for what society forced upon her; a woman of inner purity made to lead a life of outward shame?

MARCUS: What are you talking about?

REGINA: He's read a book.

MARCUS, *softly:* At nine years old I was carrying water for two bits a week. I took the first dollar I ever had and went to the paying library to buy a card. When I was twelve I was working out in the fields, and that same year I taught myself Latin and French. At fourteen I was driving mules all day and most of the night, but that was the year I learned my Greek, read my classics, taught myself— Think what I must have wanted for sons. And then think what I got. One unsuccessful trickster, one proud illiterate. No, I don't think Oscar's ever read a book.

LAVINIA: He did, Marcus. I used to read my Bible to him.

MARCUS, *to Oscar:* If you want to go away with this girl, what's detaining you?

OSCAR, *eagerly:* Your permission, sir.

MARCUS: Talk sense. Do you mean money?

OSCAR: Just a loan. Then we'd ship on down to New Orleans—

MARCUS: How much?

OSCAR: Could invest in a little business Laurette knows about— *Regina laughs loudly.* Ten thousand could start me off fine, Papa—

MARCUS: There will be a thousand dollars for you, in an envelope, on that table by six in the morning. Get on the early train. Send a Christmas card each year to an aging man who now wishes you to go upstairs.

OSCAR, *starts to protest, changes his mind:* Well, thank you. Seems kind of strange to be saying good-bye after twenty-five years—

REGINA, *gaily:* Oh, don't think of it that way. We'll be coming to see you some day. You'll have ten children, and five of the leaner ones may be yours.

LAVINIA: Good-bye, son. I'm sorry if— I'm sorry.

OSCAR: I'll write you, Mama. *To Ben, sharply:* You've bullied me since the day I was born. But before I leave—*fiercely*—you're going to do what I tell you. You're going to be on the station platform tomorrow morning. You're going to be there to apologize to Laurette.

MARCUS: Goodness, what a thousand dollars won't do!

OSCAR: And if you're not ready on time—*takes a pistol from his pocket*—I'll get you out of bed with this. And then you won't apologize to her standing up, but on your knees—

MARCUS, *violently, turning around:* Put that gun away. How dare you, in this house—

BEN, *smiles:* You've always been frightened of guns, Papa. Ever since that night, wasn't it?

LAVINIA: That's true, ever since that night.

MARCUS, *very angry:* Put that gun away. And get upstairs. Immediately.

OSCAR, *to Ben:* See you at the station. *He crosses room, exits.*

BEN, *after a second:* No need to be so nervous. I could have taken the gun away from him.

LAVINIA: And they had hot tar and clubs and ropes that night—

MARCUS: *Stop your crazy talk, Lavinia.*

LAVINIA, *softly:* I don't like that word, Marcus. No, I don't. I think you use it just to hurt my feelings.

BEN, *smiles:* He's upset, Mama. Old fears come back, strong.

MARCUS, *slowly, to Ben:* You're wearing me thin.

REGINA, *yawns:* Oh, don't you and Ben start again. *She pats Ben on the arm:* You know Papa always wins. But maybe you'll have your time some day. Try to get along, both of you. After Mama and I leave you'll be here alone together.

MARCUS: I don't know, darling. I'm going to miss you. I think I may join you.

REGINA, *turns, hesitantly:* Join me? But—

BEN: That would spoil the plan.

MARCUS, *to Regina:* I'll let you and Lavinia go ahead. Then I'll come and get you and we'll take a turn in New York. And then Regina and I will go on to Europe and you'll come back here, Lavinia.

LAVINIA: Oh, Marcus, you just can't have been listening to me. I been telling you since yesterday, and for years before *that*—

MARCUS, *looks at Regina:* You want me to come, darling?

REGINA, *nervously:* Of course. When were you thinking of coming, Papa? Soon or—

BEN, *to Regina—laughs:* I'm dying to see you get out of this one, honey.

MARCUS, *angrily, to Ben:* What are you talking about?

BEN: I'm going to be sorry to miss the sight of your face when Regina produces the secret bridegroom. *Marcus wheels to stare at Regina.* Oh, you know about it. You guessed tonight. Captain Bagtry. I don't think he wants to marry her. I don't think he even wants to sleep with her any more. But he's a weak man and— *Marcus is advancing toward him.* That won't do any good. I'm going to finish. Yesterday, if you remember,

Regina wanted you to make the loan to the girl. To-night, when she found out John Bagtry wanted to use a little of the money to leave here, and her, she talked you out of it.

REGINA: *Ben, be still.* Ben— *Goes swiftly to Marcus:* Don't listen, Papa. I have seen John, I told you that. I like him, yes. But don't you see what Ben is doing? He wanted to marry me off to money, he's angry—

BEN, *to Marcus:* I'm telling the truth. The whole town's known it for a year.

LAVINIA: Don't, Benjamin, don't! Marcus, you look so bad—

BEN: You do look bad. Go up to him, Regina, put your arms around him. Tell him you've never really loved anybody else, and never will. Lie to him, just for to-night. Tell him you'll never get in bed with anybody ever again—

Marcus slaps Ben sharply across the face.

LAVINIA, *desperately:* God help us! Marcus! Ben!

BEN, *softly:* I won't forget that. As long as I live.

MARCUS: Lock your door tonight, and be out of here before I am down in the morning. Wherever you decide to go, be sure it's far away. Get yourself a modest job, because wherever you are, I'll see to it that you never get any other.

BEN: I spent twenty years lying and cheating to help make you rich. I was trying to outwait you, Papa, but I guess I couldn't do it. *He exits.*

LAVINIA: Twenty years, he said. Then it would be my fault, my sin, too— *She starts for hall door, calling:* Benjamin! I want to talk to you, son. You're my first-born, going away—

She disappears. There is a long pause. Marcus sits down.

MARCUS: How could you let him touch you? When did it happen? How could you— *Answer me.*

REGINA, *wearily:* Are they questions that can be answered?

MARCUS: A dead man, a foolish man, an empty man from an idiot world. A man who wants nothing but war, any war, just a war. A man who believes in nothing, and never will. A man in space—

REGINA, *softly—comes to him:* All right, Papa. That's all true, and I know it. And I'm in love with him, and I want to marry him. *He puts his hands over his face. She speaks coldly.* Now don't take on so. It just won't do. You let me go away, as we planned. I'll get married. After a while we'll come home and we'll live right here—

MARCUS: *Are you crazy?* Do you think I'd stay in this house with you and—

REGINA: Otherwise, I'll go away. I say I will, and you know I will. I'm not frightened to go. But if I go that way I won't ever see you again. And you don't want that: I don't think you could stand that. My way, we can be together. You'll get used to it, and John won't worry us. There'll always be you and me— *Puts her*

hand on his shoulder. You must have known I'd marry
some day, Papa. Why, I've never seen you cry before.
It'll just be like going for a little visit, and before you
know it I'll be home again, and it will all be over. You
know? Maybe next year, or the year after, you and I'll
make that trip to Greece, just the two of us. *Smiles.*
Now it's all settled. Kiss me good night, darling. *She
kisses him, he does not move. Then she moves toward
door as Lavinia comes in.*

LAVINIA: Ben won't let me talk to him. He'd feel better
if he talked, if he spoke out— I'm his Mama and I got
to take my responsibility for what—

REGINA: Mama, I think we'll be leaving for Chicago
sooner than we thought. We'll start getting ready tomorrow morning. Good night. *She exits.*

LAVINIA, *softly, after a minute:* Did you forget to tell
her that I can't go with her? Didn't you tell them all
where I'm going? I think you better do that, Marcus—

MARCUS, *softly—very tired:* I don't feel well. Please
stop jabbering, Lavinia.

LAVINIA: You tell Regina tomorrow. You tell her how
you promised me. *Desperately:* Marcus. It's all I've
lived for. And it can't wait now. I'm getting old, and
I've got to go and do my work.

MARCUS, *wearily:* It isn't easy to live with you, Lavinia.
It really isn't. Leave me alone.

LAVINIA, *gently:* I know. We weren't ever meant to be
together. You see, being here gives me—well, I won't

use bad words, but it's always made me feel like I sinned. And God wants you to make good your sins before you die. That's why I got to go now.

MARCUS: I've stood enough of that. Please don't ever speak of it again.

LAVINIA: Ever speak of it? But you swore to me over and over again.

MARCUS: Did you ever think I meant that nonsense?

LAVINIA: But I'm going!

MARCUS: You're never going. Dr. Seckles knows how strange you've been, the whole town knows you're crazy. Now I don't want to listen to any more of that talk ever. I try to leave you alone, try to leave me alone. If you worry me any more with it, I'll have to talk to the doctor and ask him to send you away. *Softly—crying:* Please go to bed now, and don't walk around all night again.

LAVINIA, *stares at him:* Coralee. . . . Coralee! He never ever meant me to go. He says I can't go. Coralee— *She starts to move slowly, then she begins to run.* Coralee, are you in bed—

CURTAIN

ACT THREE

SCENE: *Same as Act One, early the next morning. At rise of curtain, Lavinia is moving about in the living room.*

LAVINIA, *singing:*
> Got one life, got to hold it bold
> Got one life, got to hold it bold
> Lord, my year must come.

She comes on the porch. She is carrying a small Bible.
> Got one life, got to hold it bold
> Got one life, got to hold it bold
> Lord, my year must come.

Ben, carrying a valise, comes from the living room. Lavinia gets up.

LAVINIA: All night I been waiting. You wouldn't let your Mama talk to you.

BEN: I put all my stuff in the ironing room. I'll send for it when I find a place.

LAVINIA, *softly:* Take me with you, son. As far as Alta-loosa. There I'll get off, and there I'll stay. Benjamin, he couldn't bring me back, or send me, or do, or do. He couldn't, if you'd protect me for a while and—

BEN: I, protect you? *Smiles.* Didn't you hear him last night? Don't you know about me?

LAVINIA: I don't know. I heard so much. I get mixed. I know you're bad off now. *She reaches up as if to touch his face.* You're my first-born, so it must be my fault some way.

BEN: Do you like me, Mama?

LAVINIA, *after a second:* Well. You've grown away from— I loved you, Benjamin.

BEN, *turns away:* Once upon a time.

LAVINIA: Take me with you. Take me where I can do my little good. The colored people are forgiving people. And they'll help me. You know, I should have gone after that night, but I stayed for you children. I didn't know then that none of you would ever need a Mama. Well, I'm going now. *I tell you I'm going. Her voice rises.* I spoke with God this night, in prayer. He said I should go no matter. Strait are the gates, He said. Narrow is the way, Lavinia, He said—

BEN, *sharply:* Mama! You're talking loud. *Turns to her:* Go to bed now. You've had no sleep. I'm late. *Starts to move.*

LAVINIA: Take me, Benjamin!

BEN, *sharply:* Now go in to Coralee before you get yourself in bad shape and trouble.

LAVINIA: You've got to take me. Last night he said he'd never ever meant me to go. Last night he said if ever, then he'd have Dr. Seckles, have him, have him— *Turns, her fist clenched.* Take me away from here. For ten years he swore, for ten years he swore a lie to me. I told God about that last night, and God's message said, "Go, Lavinia, even if you have to tell the awful truth. If there is no other way, tell the truth."

BEN, *turns slightly:* The truth about what?

LAVINIA: I think, now, I should have told the truth that night. But you don't always know how to do things when they're happening. It's not easy to send your own husband into a hanging rope.

BEN: What do you mean?

LAVINIA: All night long I been thinking I should go right up those steps and tell him what I know. Then he'd have to let me leave or— *Puts her hands to her face.* I've always been afraid of him, because once or twice—

BEN: Of course. But you're not afraid of me.

LAVINIA: Oh, I been afraid of you, too. I spent a life afraid. And you know that's funny, Benjamin, because way down deep I'm a woman wasn't made to be afraid. What are most people afraid of? Well, like your Papa, they're afraid to die. But I'm not afraid to die because my colored friends going to be right there to pray me in.

BEN, *carefully:* Mama, what were you talking about? Telling the truth, a hanging rope—

LAVINIA: And if you're not afraid of dying then you're not afraid of anything. *Sniffs the air.* The river's rising. I can tell by the azalea smell—

BEN, *tensely, angrily:* For God's sake, Mama, try to remember what you were saying, if you were saying anything.

LAVINIA: I was saying a lot. I could walk up those steps and tell him I could still send him into a hanging rope unless he lets me go: I could say I saw him that night, and I'll just go and tell everybody I did see him—

BEN: *What night?*

LAVINIA: The night of the massacre, of course.

BEN, *tensely, sharply:* Where did you see him, how—

LAVINIA: You being sharp with me now. And I never been sharp with you. Never—

BEN, *carefully:* Mama. Now listen to me. It's late and there isn't much time. I'm in trouble, bad trouble, and you're in bad trouble. Tell me fast what you're talking about. Maybe I can get us both out of trouble. Maybe. But only if you tell me now. *Now.* And tell me quick and straight. You can go away and I—

LAVINIA, *rises:* I saw him, like I told you, the night of the massacre, on the well-house roof.

BEN: All right. I understand what you mean. All right. But there's a lot I don't know or understand.

LAVINIA, *as if she hadn't heard him:* One time last night, I thought of getting his envelope of money, bringing it out here, tearing it up, and watching his face when he saw it at breakfast time. But it's not nice to see people grovel on the ground for money—

BEN: The envelope of money? The little envelope of money or the big envelope?

LAVINIA: I could get it, tear it up.

BEN, *carefully:* Why not? Get it now and just tear it up.

LAVINIA: And I thought too about giving it to the poor. But it's evil money and not worthy of the poor.

BEN: No, the poor don't want evil money. That's not the way.

LAVINIA, *turns to him:* Oh, I am glad to hear you say that, but you can see how I have been tempted when I thought what the money could do for my little school. I want my colored children to have many things.

BEN, *desperately:* You can have everything for them if—

LAVINIA: Oh, nobody should have everything. All I want is a nice school place, warm in winter, and a piano, and books and a good meal every day, hot and fattening.

BEN, *comes to her, stands in front of her:* Get up, Mama. Come here. He'll be awake soon. *Lavinia rises, he takes her by the arms.* Papa will be awake soon.

LAVINIA, *looks at him, nods:* First part of the war I was so ill I thought it was brave of your Papa to run the blockade, even though I knew he was dealing with the enemy to do it. People were dying for salt and I thought it was good to bring it to them. I didn't know he was getting eight dollars a bag for it, Benjamin, a little bag. Imagine taking money for other people's misery.

BEN, *softly:* Yes, I know all that, Mama. Everybody does now.

LAVINIA, *puzzled:* But I can't tell what you know, Benjamin. You were away in New Orleans in school and it's hard for me to put in place what you know and— *Ben moves impatiently.* So—well, there was the camp where our boys were being mobilized. It was up the river, across the swamp fork, back behind the old delta fields.

BEN: Yes, I know where it was. And I know that Union troops crossed the river and killed the twenty-seven boys who were training there. And I know that Papa was on one of his salt-running trips that day and that every man in the county figured Union troops couldn't have found the camp unless they were led through to it, and I know they figured Papa was the man who did the leading.

LAVINIA: He didn't lead them to the camp. Not on purpose. No, Benjamin, I am sure of that.

BEN: I agree with you. It wouldn't have paid him enough, and he doesn't like danger. So he didn't do it.

And he proved to them he wasn't here so he couldn't have done it. *Turns to her:* So now where are we?

LAVINIA: They were murder mad the night they found the poor dead boys. They came with hot tar and guns to find your Papa.

BEN, *softly:* But they didn't find him.

LAVINIA: But I found him. *She opens the Bible, holds it up, peers at it. Ben comes toward her.* At four-thirty o'clock Coralee and I saw him and heard him, on the well-house roof. We knew he kept money and papers there, and so we guessed right away where to look, and there he was.

BEN, *looks at her, smiles, softly:* And there he was.

LAVINIA: So you see I hadn't told a lie, Benjamin. He wasn't ever in the *house.* But maybe half a lie is worse than a real lie.

BEN, *quickly:* Yes, yes. Now how did he get away, and how did he prove to them—

LAVINIA: Coralee and I sat on the wet ground, watching him. Oh, it was a terrible thing for me. It was a wet night and Coralee caught cold. I had to nurse her for days afterward, with—

BEN, *looks up at balcony: Mama!* It's got to be quick now. Shall I tell you why? I've got to go unless— Now tell me how did he get away, and how did he prove to them that all the time he had been down Mobile road?

LAVINIA, *opens her Bible:* Twenty minutes to six he

climbed down from the roof, unlocked the well-house door, got some money from the envelope, and went on down through the back pines. Coralee and I ran back to the house, shivering and frightened. I didn't know what was going to happen, so we locked all the doors and all the windows and Coralee coughed, and sneezed, and ran a fever.

BEN, *angrily:* I don't give a damn about Coralee's health.

LAVINIA, *gently:* That's the trouble with you, Benjamin. You don't ever care about other folks.

There is the sound of a door closing inside the house.

BEN, *quietly:* *There is not much time left now. Try, Mama, try hard.* Tell me how he managed.

LAVINIA, *looks down at the Bible:* Well, three days later, no, two days later, the morning of April 5, 1864, at exactly ten-five—

BEN, *sharply:* What are you reading?

LAVINIA: He rode back into town, coming up Mobile road. They were waiting for him and they roped him and searched him. But he had two passes proving he had ridden through Confederate lines the day before the massacre, and didn't leave till after it. The passes were signed by—*looks at Bible*—Captain Virgil E. Mc-Mullen of the 5th Tennessee from Memphis. They were stamped passes, they were good passes, and they had to let him go. But he had no money when he came home. So Coralee and I just knew he paid Captain Virgil E.

McMullen to write those passes. *Looks down at book:*
Virgil E. McMullen, Captain in the 5th Tennessee—

BEN, *tensely—points to Bible:* It's written down there?

LAVINIA: Coralee and I were half wild with what was
the right thing to do and the wrong. So we wrote it all
down here in my Bible and we each put our hand on
the Book and swore to it. That made us feel better—

BEN: I'm sure of it. Give me the Bible, Mama—

LAVINIA: I think there's one in your room, at least there
used to be—

BEN: Oh, Mama. For God's sake. I need it. It's the
only proof we've got, and even then he'll—

LAVINIA: You don't need half this proof. That's the
trouble with your kind of thinking, Benjamin. My, I
could just walk down the street, tell the story to the
first people I met. They'd believe me, and they'd believe Coralee. We're religious women and everybody
knows it. *Smiles.* And then they'd want to believe us,
nothing would give them so much pleasure as, as, as,
well, calling on your Papa. I think people always believe what they want to believe, don't you? I don't think
I'd have any trouble, if you stood behind me, and gave
me courage to do the right talking.

BEN, *laughs:* I'll be behind you. But I'd like the Bible
behind me. Come, Mama, give it to me now. I need it
for us. *Slowly she hands the Bible to him.* All right.
Now I'd like to have that envelope.

LAVINIA: But what has the money got to do with—I

don't understand why the envelope—I'm trying hard to understand everything, but I can't see what it has—

BEN: I can't either. So let's put it this way: it would make me feel better to have it. There's nothing makes you feel better at this hour of the morning than an envelope of money.

LAVINIA, *thinks:* Oh. Well. *Points into living room:* It's in the small upper left-hand drawer of your Papa's desk. But I don't know where he keeps the key.

BEN, *laughs:* That's very negligent of you. We won't need the key. *Takes her hand, takes her under balcony.* Now call Papa. I'll be back in a minute.

LAVINIA: Oh, I couldn't do that. I never have—

BEN, *softly:* You're going to do a lot of things you've never done before. Now I want you to do what I tell you, and trust me from now on, will you?

LAVINIA: I'm going to do what you tell me.

BEN, *goes into living room:* All right. Now go ahead.

Jake appears. He is carrying a mop and a pail.

JAKE: You all up specially early, or me, am I late?

LAVINIA, *calling:* Marcus. Marcus. *To Jake:* What do you think of that, Jake?

JAKE, *takes a nervous step toward her—softly:* I don't think well of it. Please, Miss Viney, don't be doing—

LAVINIA: Marcus! Marcus! I want—we want to speak

to you. *To Jake:* Hear what I did? *Nervously:* Everything's different—Marcus!

Marcus appears on the porch. He has been dressing; he is now in shirtsleeves. He peers down at Lavinia.

MARCUS: Are you shouting at me? What's the matter with you now, Lavinia?

LAVINIA: Well, I just—

MARCUS: You are up early to give your blessings to your departing sons?

LAVINIA: I haven't seen Oscar.

MARCUS: Benjamin has gone?

LAVINIA, *looks into drawing room:* No, Marcus. He hasn't gone. He's inside knocking off the locks on your desk. My, he's doing it with a pistol. The other end of the pistol, I mean.

During her speech, we hear three rapid, powerful blows. Marcus grips the rail of the porch. Ben comes onto the porch, the pistol in one hand, a large envelope in the other. He looks up at Marcus. There is a long pause.

MARCUS: Put the gun on the table. Bring me that envelope.

LAVINIA: Same old envelope. Like I said, I used to dream about tearing up that money. You could do it, Benjamin, right now. Make you feel better and cleaner, too.

BEN: I feel fine. *To Marcus:* I like you better up there. So stay there. *Stay there.   Ben turns to Jake, takes an-*

other envelope from his pocket, puts in money from first envelope. Take this over to Lionnet. Ask for Miss Birdie Bagtry and talk to nobody else. Give her this and ask her to forget about last night.

MARCUS: Take that envelope from him, Lavinia, and bring it to me quickly.

LAVINIA: I can't walk as fast as I used to, Marcus, I'm getting old—

BEN, *to Jake:* Tell Miss Birdie I'll call on her in the next few days and we'll attend to the details then. Go on, be quick—

MARCUS, *to Jake:* Come back here! *To Ben:* How dare you touch—

BEN: Well, come and get it from me. *Turns again to Jake:* And tell her I wish Captain Bagtry good luck. And stop at the wharf and buy two tickets on the sugar boat.

LAVINIA: Thank you, son. *There is a long pause. She is puzzled by it.* Well. Why doesn't somebody say something?

BEN: We're thinking.

MARCUS: Yes. Shall I tell you what I'm thinking? That I'm going to be sorry for the scandal of a son in jail.

BEN: What would you put me in jail for?

MARCUS: For stealing forty thousand dollars.

BEN, *looking at the envelope, smiles:* That much? I haven't had time to count it. I always said there wasn't a Southerner, born before the war, who ever had sense enough to trust a bank. Now do you want to know what *I'm* thinking?

MARCUS: Yes, I'm puzzled. This piece of insanity isn't like you. In the years to come, when I do think about you, I would like to know why you walked yourself into a jail cell.

BEN: In the years to come, when you think about me, do it this way. *Sharply:* You had been buying salt from the Union garrison across the river. On the morning of April 2nd you rode over to get it. Early evening of April 3rd you started back with it—

MARCUS: Are you writing a book about me? I would not have chosen you as my recorder.

BEN: You were followed back—which is exactly what Union officers had been waiting for—at eleven o'clock that night—

LAVINIA: Marcus didn't *mean* to lead them back. I explained that to you, Benjamin—

MARCUS, *sharply:* *You* explained it to him? What—

BEN: Eleven o'clock that night twenty-seven boys in the swamp camp were killed. The news reached here, and you, about an hour later.

LAVINIA: More than that. About two hours later. Or maybe more, Benjamin.

MARCUS: What the hell is this? Lavinia, I want—

BEN: And the town, guessing right, and hating you anyway, began to look for you. They didn't find you. Because you were on the well-house roof.

LAVINIA: Yes you were, Marcus, that's just where you were. I saw you.

MARCUS, *softly:* I don't know why I'm standing here listening to this foolishness, and I won't be for long. Bring me the envelope, and you will still have plenty of time to catch the train. You come up here, Lavinia—

BEN: I'll tell you why you're standing there: you are very, very, very—as Mama would say—afraid.

MARCUS, *carefully:* What should I be afraid of, Benjamin? *Sharply:* A bungler who leaves broken locks on a desk to prove he's stolen, and gives away money to make sure I have further proof? Or a crazy woman, who dreams she saw something sixteen years ago?

LAVINIA: Marcus, I must ask you to stop using that awful word and—

MARCUS: And I must ask you to get used to it because within an hour you'll be where they use no other word—

BEN, *as Lavinia makes frightened motion:* Mama, stop it. *To Marcus:* And you stop interrupting me. Mama saw you on the well-house roof. Coralee saw you. They saw you take money from an envelope—

LAVINIA: The same one. My, it wore well, didn't it?

BEN: To buy the passes that saved you from a hanging. You bought them from—

MARCUS, *tensely:* Get out of here. I—

BEN: From a Captain Virgil E. McMullen. Now I'd figure it this way: by the grace of Captain McMullen you got sixteen free years. So if they swing you tonight, tell yourself sixteen years is a long time, and lynching is as good a way to die as any other.

LAVINIA: Benjamin, don't talk like that, don't, son—

MARCUS, *in a different voice:* Walk yourself down to the sheriff's office now. I'll catch up with you. If you're fool enough to believe some invention of your mother's, understand that nobody else will believe it. The whole town knows your mother's been crazy for years, and Dr. Seckles will testify to it—

BEN: Let's put it this way: they think Mama is an eccentric, and that you made her that way. And they know Seckles is a drunken crook. They know Mama is a good woman, they respect her. They'll take her word because, as she told me a little while ago, people believe what they want to believe.

MARCUS, *carefully:* Lavinia, you're a religious woman, and religious people don't lie, of course. But I know you are subject to dreams. Now, I wonder why and when you had this one. Remember, will you, that you were ill right after the incident of which you speak so incorrectly, and remember please that we took you— *sharply, to Ben*—not to that drunken Seckles, but to

Dr. Hammanond in Mobile. He told me then that you were— *Lavinia draws back.* And he is still living to remember it, if you can't.

LAVINIA, *worried, rattled:* I was ill after that night. Who wouldn't have been? It had nothing to do with, with my nerves. It was taking part in sin, your sin, that upset me, and not knowing the right and wrong of what to do—

MARCUS: She didn't tell you about that illness, did she? You think they'd believe her against Hammanond's word that she was a very sick woman at the time she speaks about? *Very sharply:* Now stop this damned nonsense and get out of here or—

BEN: Go change your dress, Mama. Get ready for a walk.

LAVINIA: But you told Jake—you said I could go on the sugar boat.

BEN: You can still catch the boat. We won't be walking long. And if you have to stay over a few hours more, I figure you can wear the same costume to a lynching as you can on a boat. We'll walk around to old Isham first, whose youngest son got killed that night. John Bagtry will be mighty happy to remember that his twin brother also died that night. And Mrs. Mercer's oldest son and the two Sylvan boys and— We won't have to go any further because they'll be glad to fetch their kinfolk and, on their way, all the people who got nothing else to do tonight, or all the people who owe you on cotton or cane or land. Be the biggest, happiest

lynching in the history of Roseville County. All right.
Go change your clothes—

MARCUS, *softly, carefully:* Lavinia. I—

LAVINIA: A lynching? *I don't believe in lynching.* If you
lynch a white man, it can lead right into lynching a
black man. No human being's got a right to take a life,
in the sight of God.

MARCUS, *to Ben:* You're losing your witness. What a
clown you turned out to be. Only you would think your
mother would go through with this, only you would
trust her—

BEN, *sharply:* She won't have to do much. I'm taking
her Bible along. *Opens the book:* On this page, that
night, she wrote it all down. The names, the dates, the
hours. Then she and Coralee swore to it. Everybody
will like the picture of the two lost innocents and a
Bible, and if they don't, sixteen-year-old ink will be
much nicer proof than your Mobile doctor. *Softly:* Anyway, you won't have time to get him here. Want to
finish now?

LAVINIA, *who has been thinking:* I never told you I was
going to have anything to do with a lynching. No, I
didn't.

MARCUS: Of course you wouldn't. Of course you
wouldn't. Not of your husband—

LAVINIA: Not of my husband, not of anybody.

BEN: Mama, go upstairs and let me finish this—

LAVINIA: I only said I was going to tell the truth to everybody. And that I'm going to do. *To Marcus:* If there's any nasty talk of lynching, I'm going to plead for your life hard as I can, yes I am.

BEN, *laughs:* Now, that's merciful of you. I'm going to do the same thing. I'm going to plead with them for Papa's life.

LAVINIA: That's the least a son can do for his father.

BEN, *to Marcus:* Better than that. I'll come tomorrow morning and cut you down from the tree, and bury you with respect. How did the Greeks bury fathers who were murdered? Tell me, and I'll see to it. You'd like that, wouldn't you?

LAVINIA: Benjamin, don't talk that way—

MARCUS: You gave him the right to talk that way. You did, Lavinia, and I don't understand anything that's been happening. Do you mean that you actually wrote a lie in your Bible, you who—

LAVINIA, *very angry:* Don't you talk like that. Nobody can say there's a lie in my Bible— You take that back. You take it back right away. I don't tell lies, and then I don't swear to them, and I don't swear on my Bible to a false thing and neither does Coralee. You just apologize to me and then you apologize to Coralee, that's what you do—

MARCUS, *quickly:* No, no. I don't mean you knew it was a lie. Of course not, Lavinia. But let me see it, and then tell me—

LAVINIA, *puts out her hand:* Let him see it. Of course.

BEN: Tell him to come down and look at it. I'll put it here, under the gun.

LAVINIA: Bibles are there for all people. For grown people. I'm not going to have any Bibles in my school. That surprise you all? It's the only book in the world but it's just for grown people, after you know it don't mean what it says. You take Abraham: he sends in his wife, Sarah, to Pharaoh, and he lets Pharaoh think Sarah is his sister. And then Pharaoh, he, he, he. Well, he does, with Sarah. And afterward Abraham gets mad at Pharaoh because of Sarah, even though he's played that trick on Pharaoh. Now if you didn't understand, a little child could get mighty mixed up—

MARCUS, *gently:* You want to go to your school, don't you, Lavinia?

LAVINIA: Or about Jesus. The poor are always with you. Why, I wouldn't have colored people believe a thing like that: that's what's the matter now. You have to be full grown before you know what Jesus meant. Otherwise you could make it seem like people ought to be poor.

BEN: All right. Go upstairs now and start packing. You're going to be on the sugar boat.

LAVINIA: Am I? Isn't that wonderful—

MARCUS: Lavinia. *She turns toward him.* It would be wrong of me to say ours had been a good marriage. But a marriage it was. And you took vows in church, sacred vows. If you sent me to trouble, you would be breaking your sacred vows—

BEN: Oh, shut up, Papa.

LAVINIA: I don't want trouble, for anybody. I've only wanted to go away—

MARCUS, *slowly, as he comes down from balcony:* I was wrong in keeping you.

BEN, *laughs:* Yes. That's true.

MARCUS: It was wrong, I can see it now, to have denied you your great mission. I should have let you go, helped you build you a little schoolhouse in Altaloosa.

BEN: I built it about ten minutes ago.

LAVINIA: What? Oh, about the marriage vows, Marcus. I had a message last night, and it said it was right for me to go now and do my work. Once I get a message, you know.

MARCUS: Yes. Yes, you'll want a lot of things for your colored pupils. A schoolhouse isn't enough—you'll need books and—

LAVINIA: That's absolutely true. And I want to send for a teacher— I'm getting old and I'm ignorant— I want to make a higher learning.

MARCUS: Lavinia. I'll get them for you.

LAVINIA: Thank you. But of course, it isn't just getting them, I've got to keep up the schoolhouse every year—

MARCUS: Certainly. Did your, did your messages suggest any definite figure?

LAVINIA: Why, yes, they did.

MARCUS: How much was suggested?

LAVINIA: To tell you the truth, my message said a thousand dollars a year would make my colored children happy. But I think ten thousand a year would make them happier. Altaloosa's a mighty poor little village and everybody needs help there—

MARCUS: Ten thousand wouldn't be enough. I think—

LAVINIA, *firmly:* It would be enough. I'd make it enough. Then, of course, I been forgetting about Coralee coming with me. And Coralee supports a mighty lot of kinfolk right here in town. She got a crippled little cousin, her old Mama can't take washing any more—

MARCUS: Oh, that's too bad. What could I do for them?

LAVINIA: Maybe two hundred dollars a month would take Coralee's mind from worrying.

MARCUS: I should think so. They'll be the richest family in the South. But, of course, your friends should have the best.

LAVINIA: You're being mighty nice to me, Marcus. I wish it had always been that way.

MARCUS, *quickly:* It started out that way, remember? I suppose little things happened, as they do with so many people—

LAVINIA: No, I don't really think it started out well. No, I can't say I do.

MARCUS: Oh, come now. You're forgetting. All kinds of pleasant things. Remember in the little house? The piano? I saved and bought it for you and—

LAVINIA: Bought it for me? No, I don't remember it that way. I always thought you bought it for yourself.

MARCUS: But perhaps you never understood why I did anything, perhaps you were a little unforgiving with me.

BEN, *to Marcus:* Aren't you getting ashamed of yourself?

MARCUS: For what? For trying to recall to Lavinia's mind that we were married with sacred vows, that together we had children, that she swore in a church to love, to honor—

BEN: If I wasn't in a hurry, I'd be very amused.

LAVINIA, *thoughtfully:* I did swear. That's true, I—

BEN, *quickly:* Mama, please go upstairs. Please let me finish here. You won't get on the boat any other way—

MARCUS: Indeed you will, Lavinia. And there's no need to take the boat. I'll drive you up. We can stay overnight in Mobile, look at the churches, have a nice dinner, continue on in the morning—

LAVINIA: How did you guess? I always dreamed of returning that way. Driving in, nice and slow, seeing everybody on the road, saying hello to people I knew as

a little girl, stopping at the river church—church . . .
To herself: Every Sunday here I always saved and put
a dollar in the collection box. They're going to miss
the dollar. You all know, in my vanity, what I'd like to
have when I'm gone to Altaloosa?

MARCUS: What, Lavinia? I am most anxious to know.

LAVINIA: A mahogany pew, with my name on it, in
brass.

MARCUS: Brass! It shall be writ in gold—

LAVINIA: I don't like gold. Brass. Now, what else did I
think about last night?

MARCUS: We'll be in constant communication. And if
you have more practical messages from God we can
take care of them later. Now bring me the envelope and
the Bible, and we'll start immediately—

She puts her hand on the Bible, as if to pick it up.

BEN, *quickly takes her hand:* Do I really have to explain it to you? Do I really have to tell you that unless
you go through with it, he's got to take you to the hospi-
tal? You don't really think that he's going to leave
you free in Altaloosa with what you know, to tell anybody— Why do you think he took you to Dr. Hammanond in the first place? Because he thought you
might have seen him, and because it wouldn't hurt to
have a doctor say that you were—

MARCUS, *very sharply:* That's a lie.

BEN: Maybe it is. But then you're only sorry you didn't
think of it that way.

MARCUS: Lavinia—

LAVINIA, *softly:* I don't ever want to hear such things again, or one person do or say, to another.

MARCUS: Lavinia, you'll get what you want. You know I am not a stingy man or one who—

BEN: You'll get nothing. For the very simple reason that he isn't going to have a nickel to buy it with.

LAVINIA, *wearily:* Oh. That isn't what worries me— It's that Marcus may have been saying things he didn't mean. *Softly:* Would you really have told me you would drive me to Mobile and then you would have taken me—

MARCUS: *Of course not.* If you listen to that scoundrel— You're my wife, aren't you? I also took vows. I also stood up and swore. Would I break a solemn vow—

LAVINIA, *appalled:* Oh, now, I don't believe what you're saying. One lie, two lies, that's for all of us: but to pile lie upon lie and sin upon sin, and in the sight of God—

BEN, *sharply:* Write it to him, Mama. Or you'll miss your boat.

LAVINIA: Oh, yes. Oh, I wouldn't want to do that. *She picks up the Bible, exits.*

MARCUS: You're a very ugly man.

BEN: Are you ready now?

MARCUS: For what?

BEN: To write a piece of paper, saying you sell me the store for a dollar.

MARCUS, *pauses:* All right. Bring me that envelope. I'll sell you the store for a dollar. Now I have had enough and that will be all.

BEN: You'll write another little slip of paper telling Shannon in Mobile to turn over to me immediately all stocks and bonds, your safe-deposit box, all liens, all mortgages, *all* assets of Marcus Hubbard, Incorporated.

MARCUS: I will certainly do no such thing. I will leave you your proper share of things in my will, or perhaps increase it, if you behave—

BEN, *angrily:* You're making fun of me again. A will? That you could change tomorrow? You've made fun of me for enough years. It's dangerous now. One more joke. So stop it now. Stop it.

MARCUS: All right. But I would like to give you a little advice—you're so new at this kind of thing. If you get greedy and take everything there's bound to be a lot of suspicion. And you shouldn't want that. Take the store, take half of everything else, half of what's in the envelope. Give me the rest. I'll go on living as I always have, and tell everybody that because you're my oldest son, I wanted you to have—

BEN: You'll tell nobody anything, because you can't, and you'll stop bargaining. You're giving me everything you've got. Is that clear? If I don't have to waste any more time with you, I'll give you enough to live on,

here or wherever you want to go. But if I have to talk
to you any longer, you won't get that. I mean what I'm
saying, and you know I do. And it's the last time I'll say
it. *There is no answer. He smiles.* All right. Now start
writing things down. When you finish, bring them to
me. You're waiting for something?

MARCUS, *softly, as he goes up the porch steps:* To tell
you the truth, I am trying to think of some way out.

BEN: If I told you that it's been a large temptation to
see you—to do it the other way, you will believe me, I
know; remember the past and don't waste your time, or
put yourself in further danger, or tempt me longer.
Ever since you started your peculiar way of treating me,
many years ago, I have had many ugly dreams. But this
is better than I ever dreamed— Go in and start writing
now. I consider you a lucky man: you'll die in bed.

MARCUS: You will give me enough for a clean bed?

BEN: Yes, of course.

MARCUS: Well, I daresay one could make some small
bargains with you still. But I don't like small bargains.
You win or you lose—

BEN: And I don't like small talk. *Marcus turns, goes
into his room. Ben waits for a second, then crosses to
kitchen door, calls in:* Breakfast here, please. *As Jake
comes from street side of porch:* Yes? Did you find Miss
Birdie?

JAKE: Yes, sir. She was mighty happy and said to thank
you.

BEN: All right. Did you get the tickets?

JAKE: Sure. Boat's loading now.

BEN, *sits down at Marcus's table:* Take them up to Miss Lavinia, get the carriage ready. Get me coffee first.

JAKE, *as he goes off:* Lot of running around this morning.

The sound of knocking is heard from the hall of the second floor.

OSCAR'S VOICE, *with the knocking:* Papa! Papa! It's me. Hey, Papa. Please. Open your door. *After a second Oscar runs in from the living room, runs up the porch steps, calls into Marcus's room:* Papa. I'm all ready. *Pounds on Marcus's door.*

BEN, *looking up at Oscar:* Traveling clothes? You look nice.

OSCAR: What you doing there? I told you to get on down to the station to make your apologies. I ain't changed my mind.

BEN: Oh, I never thought you meant that silly talk.

OSCAR: You didn't, huh? *Looks down, sees the gun on the table:* What's my pistol doing out?

BEN: Waiting for you.

OSCAR: You just put it back where you found it— *Then as if he remembered:* Papa. Please. Let me in. *Please.* Papa, I can't find it. Papa— *Regina appears on the balcony. She is arranging her hair. She has on a riding skirt and shirt.* Regina, go in and tell him, will you? *Please, Regina.* Laurette's waiting for me to fetch her up—

REGINA, *looks down at Ben on the porch. Looks at Oscar:* Oh, God. I slept late, hoping you'd both be gone. What's the matter with you, Oscar, what are you carrying on about?

Jake appears with coffee tray, brings cup to Ben, puts tray down, and exits.

OSCAR, *desperately:* The thousand dollars on the table. But it's *not* on the table. You heard him promise last night—

REGINA: Go look again. Papa certainly wouldn't stop your going.

OSCAR: I tell you it's not there. I been over the whole house. I crawled around under the table—

BEN: Come on down and crawl some more.

REGINA, *softly:* You're in Papa's chair, Ben, eating breakfast at Papa's table, on Papa's porch.

OSCAR, *softly, very puzzled:* I'm telling you that Ben is a crazy Mama's crazy son.

BEN, *looks up at Regina:* Come on down and have breakfast with me, darling. I'm lonely for you.

REGINA: Papa told you to be out of here.

BEN, *smiles:* Come on down, honey.

REGINA: No, I'm going out before the horse-whipping starts.

BEN: Going to look for a man who needs a little persuading?

REGINA: That's right.

OSCAR: Regina. Help me. It's *not* there.   *Screaming:* Papa! *Papa!*

REGINA, *disappears into her room:* Oh, stop that screaming.

OSCAR: Papa, I got to go. The money's not there. Papa, please answer me—

MARCUS, *comes out from his room:* You looking for me, son? Speak up.

OSCAR, *softly:* It's getting late. The money. You forgot to leave it. *When he gets no answer, his voice changes to a sudden shriek:* It just ain't there.

MARCUS: A voice injured at your age is possibly never recovered. The money isn't there, Oscar, because I didn't put it there. *To Ben:* Would you like to give him a little—some—explanation, or will I, or—

BEN, *shakes his head:* I'm eating.

Oscar stares down at Ben, stares at Marcus.

MARCUS, *to Oscar:* An unhappy event interfered. I am thus unable to finance your first happy months in the rose-covered brothel about which you have always dreamed. I assure you I am most sorry, for many reasons, none of them having anything to do with you.

OSCAR: What the hell does all that mean? That you're *not* giving me the money to leave here—

BEN, *nods:* It means that. And it means that Papa has found a new way of postponing for a few minutes an unpleasant writing job. Go back in, Papa.

Oscar stares at Marcus, stares down at Ben. Then he suddenly runs down the steps, off the porch, going toward the street. Ben smiles, Marcus smiles.

MARCUS: Where would you prefer me to have breakfast? A tray in my room, this side of the porch, or the dining room or—

BEN: Any place you like. My house is your house.

MARCUS: I eat a large breakfast, as you know. Should that continue?

BEN: Certainly. But before you eat this large breakfast, on this large morning, I want you to finish the papers I'm waiting for.

MARCUS: Naturally, I've been inside thinking. Is there any chance I could get out of here and on the train without your interfering with me?

BEN: No, I don't think so. I've thought of that. And if you did, I feel confident I could bring you back.

MARCUS, *pleasantly:* Yes. Thank you, Benjamin.

He re-enters his room as Regina comes on the porch. She hears his last sentence, stares at Marcus. She comes

*down the steps, goes to the table, pours herself coffee,
takes a biscuit, looks curiously at Ben and sits down.*

REGINA, *after a minute:* What's the matter with Papa?

BEN: He's changed. You think it's age?

REGINA, *annoyed:* Why aren't you getting on the train?

BEN: I'm going to build a new house. I never liked this
house; it wasn't meant for people like us. Too delicate,
too fancy. Papa's idea of postwar swell.

REGINA, *stares at him:* I want to know why you aren't
leaving this morning?

BEN: I can't tell you why. *Laughs.* My lips are sealed in
honor.

REGINA: Before there's any more trouble you better go
quiet down Mama. She's *packing.* She says she's going
to her destiny. You know what that always means. And
I'm sick of fights—

BEN: But that's where she is going.

REGINA, *bewildered:* Papa said she could go?

BEN: No . . . I said so.

REGINA: And who have you become?

BEN: A man who thinks you have handled yourself very
badly. It's a shame about you, Regina: beautiful, warm
outside, and smart. That should have made a brilliant
life. Instead, at twenty, you have to start picking up
the pieces, and start mighty fast now.

REGINA, *gets up, laughs:* I like the pieces, and I'm off to pick them up.

BEN: To try to persuade the Captain by the deed of darkness to a future legal bed? So early in the morning?

REGINA, *pleasantly, as she passes him:* I'm sure something very interesting has happened here. *Sharply. Turns to him:* But whatever it is, don't talk that way to me.

BEN: Can I talk this way? You're not going to Chicago. And for a very simple reason. Papa has no money at all—now. No money for you to travel with, or to marry with, or even to go on here with.

REGINA, *stands staring at him. Then, quietly:* What are you talking about? What's happened? What's he done with his money—

BEN: Given it to me.

REGINA: Do you take that new drug I've been reading about? What would make you think he had given it to you?

BEN: You mean what were his reasons? Oh, I don't know. I'm the eldest son: isn't that the way with royalty? Maybe he could find me a Greek title— Go up and talk to him. I think he's been waiting.

Slowly she starts for the staircase. Then the speed of her movements increases, and by the time she is near the door of Marcus's room she is running. She goes into the room. Ben picks up his newspaper. There is low talk-

ing from Marcus's room. Ben looks up, smiles. After a
moment, Regina comes slowly out of Marcus's room.
She crosses porch, starts downstairs.

REGINA, *slowly:* He says there is nothing he will tell me.
He says there's nothing he can tell me. He's crying.
What does all that mean?

BEN: It means there is nothing he can tell you, and that
he's crying. Don't you feel sorry for him?

REGINA: Why can't he tell me? I'll make him—

BEN: He can't tell you, and I won't tell you. Just take
my word: you're, er, you're not well off, shall we say?

REGINA, *tensely:* What have you been doing to Papa
or—

BEN: A great deal. Whatever you think of me, honey,
you know I'm not given to this kind of joke. So take it
this way: what is in your room, is yours. Nothing else.
And save your time on the talk. No Chicago, honey. No
nothing.

REGINA: You can't stop my going, and you're not going
to stop it—

BEN: Certainly not. What people want to do, they do.
You go ahead, your own way. Ride over to your soldier.
Stand close and talk soft: he'll marry you. But do it
quickly: he was angry last night and I think he wants
to get away from you as fast as he can. Catch him quick.
Marry him this morning. Then come back here to pack
your nice Chicago clothes, and sell your pearls.

REGINA: Do you think I'm going to take your word for what's happening, or believe I can't talk Papa out of whatever you've done to him—

BEN: Believe me, you can't. Not because your charms have failed, but because there's nothing to talk him out of. I have it now, and your charms won't work on me. Money from the pearls will be plenty to take you to Brazil, and love and war will feed you. People in love should be poor.

REGINA: Ben, tell me what storm happened here this morning. Tell me so that I can—can find out what I think or—

BEN: Or if you don't want to go to the war in Brazil, stay here and starve with them at Lionnet. I'd love to see you in the house with those three ninnies, dying on the vine. Either way, he'd leave you soon enough and you'd find out there's never anybody nastier than a weak man. Hurry— Or have a cup of coffee.

REGINA, *softly, tensely:* I'll find out what's happened, and—

BEN: No you won't.

REGINA: And the day I do, I'll pay you back with carnival trimmings.

BEN: Good girl. I won't blame you. But in the meantime, learn to win, and learn to lose. And don't stand here all day losing, because it's my house now, and I don't like loser's talk.

REGINA: You've ruined everything I wanted, you've—

BEN: Now, look here. Write *him* a poem, will you? I've ruined nothing. You're not marrying a man who didn't love you. You can't go away, or at least not on my money, and therefore a willful girl can't have a willful way. You're not in love; I don't think anybody in this family can love. You're not a fool; stop talking like one. The sooner you do, the sooner I'll help you.

REGINA: You heard me say I'd pay you back for this?

BEN: All right. Be a fool.

Marcus opens his door, comes out on the porch, comes down the steps. Regina turns to look at him. Marcus comes to Ben, hands him two pieces of paper. Ben takes them, reads them. Marcus puts his hand out to take the newspaper. Ben smiles, shakes his head, Marcus quickly takes his hand away.

REGINA, *desperately, to Marcus:* You still won't tell me? You're willing to see—

MARCUS, *softly:* Regina, honey, I can't, I—

Oscar, dejected and rumpled, appears.

REGINA, *to Oscar:* Do you know what's happened here? Did you have anything to do with it?

OSCAR: What?

Regina turns away from him. Oscar sits down, puts his head in his hands.

REGINA, *after a minute:* Well, what's the matter with you then? Ben Hubbard trouble?

OSCAR: She wouldn't wait. She wouldn't even wait for a few days until Papa could give me the money again.

BEN: Again?

OSCAR: That's how much she cared for me. Wouldn't even wait. Said she was going on to New Orleans, anyway. That she'd had enough— My God, I talked and begged. I even tried to carry her off the train.

MARCUS: Oh, how unfortunate.

BEN: I think it's charming. How did you do it, Oscar?

OSCAR, *to nobody:* You know what she did? She spat in my face and screamed in front of everybody that she was glad I wasn't coming, that she had never cared for me, and had only been doing the best she could. If I didn't have the money, what the hell did she need me for?

REGINA, *sympathetic:* Spat in your face! How could she do a thing like that?

MARCUS: How does one spit in your face?

BEN: Why, I imagine the way one spits in anybody's face.

REGINA: But it's special in a railroad station. How did she do it, Oscar? You can't just up and spit—

OSCAR, *in his sorrow, spits out on the porch:* Just like that. The way you wouldn't do with a dog. And all the while yelling I was to let her alone, with everybody staring and laughing— *Marcus, Regina, and Ben laugh. Oscar rises.* So. So, making fun of me, huh?

REGINA: Now, really, Oskie, can you blame us? You on a railroad station trying to carry off a spitting—girl? You'd laugh yourself, if you didn't always have indigestion.

OSCAR, *carefully:* Your love didn't laugh. Your love, looking like a statue of Robert E. Lee. Dressed up and with his old medals all over him. *Regina rises. Marcus rises.* So you didn't know he was going on the train, huh? I thought not. So you're no better off than me, are you, with all your laughing. Sneaked out on you, did he?

REGINA: So you arranged that, too, so that I couldn't—

BEN: All right. That's enough. I'm sick of love. Both of you follow the trash you've set your hearts on, or be still about it from now on. I don't want any more of this.

OSCAR: *You* don't want any more. What the—

BEN, *to Regina:* You, early-maturing flower, can go any place you want and find what it's like to be without Papa's money. *To Oscar:* And you, lover, can follow your spitting heart and get yourself a wharf job loading bananas. Or you can stay, keep your job, settle down. I got a girl picked out for you—make yourself useful.

OSCAR, *completely bewildered, turns to Marcus:* What's he talking about, Papa? Since when—

BEN: It's not necessary to explain it to you. *To Regina:* Now, honey, about you, if you're staying. You're a scandal in this town. Papa's the only person didn't know you've been sleeping with the warrior.

MARCUS: Benjamin—

BEN, *laughs:* Papa, and Horace Giddens in Mobile. How soon he'll find out about it, I don't know. Before he does, we're taking you up to see him. You'll get engaged to him by next week, or sooner, and you'll get married in the first church we bump into. Giddens isn't bad off, and if you're lucky it'll be years before he hears about you and the Brazilian general. I don't say it's a brilliant future, but I don't say it's bad. You could have done a lot better, but girls who have been despoiled in this part of the country—

MARCUS, *softly:* You don't have to marry a man, Regina, just because— We can go away, you and I—

OSCAR, *goes toward kitchen door:* I certainly don't know what's happened here. I certainly don't. I'm hungry. *Calls in:* Where's breakfast, you all?

REGINA, *sharply:* Order breakfast for me, too, selfish.

BEN, *laughs:* That's my good girl. *Picks up the newspaper.* Nothing for anybody to be so unhappy about. You both going to do all right. I'm going to help you. I got ideas. You'll go to Chicago some day, get everything you want— Then—

REGINA, *softly:* When I'm too old to want it.

MARCUS: Regina, you didn't hear me. We could go away, you and I— I could start over again just as I started once before.

REGINA: When you did—whatever Ben made you do, did you realize what you were doing to me? Did you care?

MARCUS, *slowly:* I cared very much.

REGINA: And what good did that do?

OSCAR: Sure must have been an earthquake here since last night. You go to bed and Papa's one kind of man, and you wake up—

BEN, *reading newspaper:* They got that ad in again, Oscar. Dr. Melgoyd's "All Cure." Two bits, now, on special sale, for gentlemen only. Sluggish blood, cure for a wild manhood, nothing to be ashamed of, it says—

REGINA: He's still got the last bottle.

Jake appears with a large tray. He has on his hat and coat.

OSCAR, *annoyed:* I never bought that rot. Don't believe in it. Somebody gave it to me.

REGINA, *laughing:* That was tactless, wasn't it?

BEN: Big goings on all over the country. Railroads going across, oil, coal. I been telling you, Papa, for ten years. Things are opening up.

OSCAR, *who has started to eat:* That don't mean they're opening up in the South.

BEN: But they are. That's what nobody down here sees or understands. Now you take you, Papa. You were smart in your day and figured out what fools you lived among. But ever since the war you been too busy getting cultured, or getting Southern. A few more years and you'd have been just like the rest of them.

MARCUS, *to Jake:* Bring my breakfast, Jake.

JAKE: Belle will have to do it, Mr. Marcus. Last breakfast I can bring. I got the carriage waiting to take Miss Viney. *He exits.*

BEN: But now we'll do a little quiet investing, nothing big, because unlike Papa I don't believe in going outside your class about anything—

OSCAR, *his mouth full:* Think we've got a chance to be big rich, Ben?

BEN: I think so. All of us. I'm going to make some for you and Regina and—

Lavinia appears in the living-room door. She is carrying a purse and the Bible. Coralee is standing behind her.

LAVINIA: Well, I'm off on my appointed path. I brought you each a little something. *Goes to Regina:* This is my pin. *Regina gets up, Lavinia kisses her.* Smile, honey, you're such a pretty girl. *Goes to Oscar:* Here's my prayer book, Oscar. I had it since I was five years old. *Oscar kisses her. She goes to Ben:* I want you to have my Papa's watch, Benjamin.

BEN: Thank you, Mama. *He kisses her, she pats his arm.*

LAVINIA, *goes to Marcus:* I didn't have anything left, Marcus, except my wedding ring.

MARCUS, *gets up, smiles:* That's kind, Lavinia.

LAVINIA: Well, I guess that's all.

BEN: Mama, could I have your Bible instead of Grandpa's watch? *Marcus laughs.* It would make me happier, and I think—

MARCUS: Or perhaps you'd give it to me. I can't tell you how happy it would make me, Lavinia.

LAVINIA: Oh, I wouldn't like to give it up. This Bible's been in my Papa's family for a long time. I always keep it next to me, you all know that. But when I die, I'll leave it to you all. Coralee, you hear that? If I die before you, you bring it right back here.

CORALEE: Come on, Miss Viney.

LAVINIA: I'll be hearing from you, Benjamin?

BEN: You will, Mama. Every month. On time.

LAVINIA: Thank you, son. Thank you in the name of my colored children.

CORALEE: Miss Viney, it's late.

LAVINIA: Well. *Wistfully:* Don't be seeing me off, any of you. Coralee and I'll be just fine. I'll be thinking of you, and I'll be praying for you, all of you. Everybody needs somebody to pray for them, and I'm going to pray for you all. *Turns to Marcus:* I hope you feel better, Marcus. We got old, you and me, and— Well, I guess I just mean it's been a long time. Good-bye.

MARCUS: Good-bye, Lavinia.

Lavinia and Coralee exit. Marcus goes to sit by Regina.

MARCUS, *softly:* Pour me a cup of coffee, darling.

Regina looks at him, gets up, crosses to table, pours coffee, brings it to him. Marcus pulls forward the chair next to him. Regina ignores the movement, crosses to chair near Ben, sits down. Ben smiles.

CURTAIN FALLS